Getting to Giving

Fundraising the Entrepreneurial Way

By a Billion-Dollar Fundraiser

Howard Stevenson

With Shirley Spence

Timberline LLC
P.O. Box 639
Belmont, MA 02478
email: gettingtogiving@gmail.com
toll-free line: 855-407-4158
international line: 617-945-5724

Library of Congress cataloging information forthcoming.

ISBN: 978-0-9837486-1-8 (hc)
ISBN: 978-0-9837486-0-1 (pbk)

Printed in the United States of America

To the donors who have given me both wisdom and dollars to advance the causes I have cared about. They have taught me, supported important causes, and generally made life interesting.

To the volunteers who have inspired me with their passion and commitment.

And finally, to the professionals with whom I have worked to create meaning in my life, and in the lives of our donors.

To all of them, I say "thank you."

CONTENTS

INTRODUCTION

MY PHILANTHROPIC JOURNEY

Fundraising—I often tell people—is the best career I've ever had. Most often, I make that statement in response to an assertion like, "How can you stand to do fundraising? It's so *unpleasant*!"

Copyright Grantland Enterprises; www.grantland.net

Yes, I'll admit that it's in my nature to counter people's expectations. (I can be contrarian.) But my comment is also the absolute truth: I enjoy fundraising immensely, much more than many other things I've done in my life.

Why? For one thing, it's a team sport. I get to work with other fundraisers, many of whom are extremely generous in sharing their experience and wisdom. Nothing is quite as much fun as a high-functioning team.

But even more important, as a fundraiser, I'm *proud* of the work I'm doing. I'm supporting a cause I'm personally committed to, and I'm helping like-minded donors do the same. I get to meet donors who in many cases are fascinating and impressive individuals, and I get to talk with them in intimate ways about meaningful issues that are very important to both of us. In those circumstances—I truly believe—we are doing something, together, to make the world a better place.

That said, I can understand why fundraising has become grist for the cartoonist's mill—as you saw above, and will see sprinkled throughout this book—and why so many board members and executive directors seem to hate it. People often assume that fundraising is about hearing "no" all the time. Fundraising is time-consuming, especially for people who already have too much to do. You may feel like you're in unfamiliar, even hostile territory. And for some people, asking for money feels like begging, and no one wants to be a beggar.

Copyright Grantland Enterprises; www. grantland.net

That fear of rejection turns out to be a misapprehension. When I began fundraising, I was told to expect a 25 percent closing rate—one in four—with my major gift prospects. What I learned was that you can do far better than that—maybe three times as well—if you do it right. Those who do it right raise more money. If you've done your homework, people say "yes" more often than not, and that is tremendously satisfying. It's *measurable,* too: you know exactly how you're doing. That makes it fun.

At the end of the day, individual fundraising is about potential donors, closing rates, and average gift size. If you're talking to people who don't care about what you're doing, you're likely to be rejected. That's especially disappointing when your cause is so important to you on a personal level. On the other hand, if you're able to find the right prospects, and convince more of them to give more, you magically will raise more money... and probably have a lot more fun doing it.

MY PHILANTHROPIC HISTORY

As I see it, fundraising is a natural—almost inevitable—step along the path of my life. I was raised in a tradition of being responsible to the community. From an early age, I canvassed my neighborhood on the first Sunday of each month, collecting money from members of the church to support others. I did my share of work on the local welfare farm, and performed community service with the Boy Scouts.

These experiences helped shape my belief that philanthropy isn't a separate, walled-off part of your life; it's something you do throughout your life—even if you have lots of other demands on your time, and even if you don't have a lot of money. Tithing is part of my family tradition, and I have always given a percentage of what I make to charity. I have tried to instill this in my children, and now in my grandchildren. When they were small, they were encouraged to divide up their allowance and put some of it in each of three jars: one for spending, one for saving, and one for charity.

As I grew older and pursued my professional career, I started to see new opportunities to contribute to the greater good. Land conservation, an interest of my grandfather's, became my cause. It involved *shaping deals* and *raising money*. I was better at the first—buying land, developing properties, adding value to them—than I was at the second, mainly because I didn't know anyone with money.

I enjoyed some success, and this led to yet another new phenomenon in my life: people started to ask *me* for money. Some did it well; some did it poorly. I began thinking about that difference. What made for effective fundraising, and what made for inept fundraising?

Over much of this time, I was (among other things) a professor at Harvard Business School (HBS). I left briefly in the late 1970s, but was lured back to launch a new entrepreneurial initiative. My belief was, and still is, that *every* organization has to be entrepreneurial. Entrepreneurship is, at its heart, a field of dreams—and if you're not driven by your dreams, what's the point?

The entrepreneurial program initially focused on for-profit enterprises. Eventually, though, our faculty group offered a course in which ten of the 30 case studies that we taught were about nonprofits. (For the most part, HBS classes are group discussions focused on a story—a "case"—about an organization facing a challenge.) They were fascinating stories. I recall one in particular about a group that was promoting the economic empowerment of women in Bangladesh, and thereby helped cut infant mortality rates dramatically. I was fascinated by the consistent message emerging from our classrooms. Whether the organizations we were studying were for-profits or nonprofits, their leaders talked about the same things: choosing an opportunity, and finding the resources to pursue it.

Time passed; I got older; and it became clear to me that younger people should be running the entrepreneurship program. I therefore volunteered to become what HBS calls the "Dean of External Relations." I figured that would be both interesting and easy: give some speeches, and talk to people I enjoyed. Then the school's dean threw me a curveball: "Yes, Howard, but alongside that, I also want you to run a capital campaign." At the time, I wasn't altogether sure what that meant. But to make a long story short, I'm happy to report that we ended up raising $600 million, or about 20 percent above our target.

From there, I went "across the river"— HBS and Harvard University are separated physically by the Charles River—to participate in the larger University's fundraising efforts for two years.

At this point in my life, I estimate I've played a significant personal role in raising something north of $500 million, and I've also helped in the successful solicitation of another $2 billion. Notice that I'm reluctant to say, "*I* raised." That's because fundraising almost always is, and should be, a team effort. At HBS, I oversaw an 80-person staff, including 25 fundraisers, and led the proverbial "army of volunteers," which comprised approximately 1,000 alumni. My subsequent responsibilities at Harvard University again involved the direct oversight of a staff of 80 people—who in turn managed some 600 professional fundraisers—and the rallying of some 4,000 volunteers. In short, a large-scale and intensive effort! I also have racked up my fair share of personal fundraising time. During the HBS campaign, my approximately 1,000 one-on-one meetings earned me the nickname "Professor Road Warrior." (I wore it proudly.) In group settings, I spoke to more than 5,000 people on behalf of the effort. For me, it was a profound education in fundraising—a true immersion experience.

I should also say that the Harvard campaigns are only part of my fundraising experience, which has included much smaller organizations, a variety of causes, and a number of different roles; and led to gifts ranging from $1,000 to $125 million. At Sudbury Valley Trustees (SVT), where I served as chairperson, our staff included a lone fundraiser. At National Public Radio (NPR), where I also served as chairperson, we had a half dozen. As a board member of the Boston Ballet, I assisted with strategic planning. I have served on the CareGroup Healthcare System's finance committee. I am a strong supporter of my wife Fredi's philanthropic work, which includes SummerSearch, a leadership development program for low-income students; and the Cambridge Center for Adult Education. I have been a proud donor of both time and money to all of those causes.

In short, I've spent a lot of time being engaged directly in, and also reflecting upon, the art and science of fundraising.

WHY THIS BOOK?

For several reasons, the year 2007 was a time of deep introspection for me. I reached retirement age at HBS, and I realized that while I didn't know how to stop working, it was time for me to do something different and meaningful. HBS was kind enough to offer me a professorship on a year-to-year basis, which meant I could focus on writing and teaching about entrepreneurship. But what *else* was I going to do? It was time to pause for thought.

Then came another life-changing event. On a sunny winter day, just steps outside my HBS office, I had a cardiac arrest. Not to mince words, I died. Miraculously, a security officer and the head of buildings and grounds appeared on the scene almost immediately and began administering CPR, and trained personnel from the HBS clinic showed up with a defibrillator. I was rushed to nearby Mount Auburn Hospital by ambulance. I couldn't have been luckier. But the act of dying—even for a few moments—*really* gives you pause.

So how did I really want to be spending my time? I made lists, and writing a book about fundraising kept appearing on those lists. I was being solicited for advice on the subject by various nonprofit boards, and I was invited to speak about fundraising to a wide range of groups. I was frustrated when I saw fundraising being done badly, and nonprofits struggling unnecessarily. I was increasingly convinced of the power of philanthropy—and the need for it!—not just in the U.S., but worldwide. I saw that many "public needs" will have to call upon philanthropy as at least part of the solution. For all these reasons and more, I decided to go part-time at HBS, and devote my freed-up time to this book.

The U.S. has an outstanding tradition of philanthropy—a tradition that is rooted in our frontier history. Back in those early days, if you fell on hard times, there was no powerful king, or great church, or even an effective local government in a position to help you very much. You had to hope that individuals or groups in the community would step forward to lend you a hand. Yes, in the intervening centuries, philanthropy has become far more professionalized. At the end of the day, though, it is still an intensely *personal* act. It's voluntary, and flies in the face of a basic economic principle: nobody gives up personal resources without getting something tangible in return, right? Wrong. Lots of people do.

Happily, philanthropy has moved far beyond U.S. borders and traditions. Philanthropic giving is becoming an increasingly important economic force around the world. One reason is that governments have taken on more and more activities that they now can't pay for. Cutbacks are reducing social services even as *needs continue to grow*. The good news is that philanthropic organizations tend to spring up to fill those gaps.

But that dynamic, in turn, creates a whole new set of problems. The apparent competition for philanthropic resources has intensified. (Though my belief is that organizations with common values and goals should work together, not compete.) Nonprofits are escalating their fundraising activities. As individuals, we are barraged by compelling appeals for aid from local, national, and international organizations; by phone, mail, and Internet. I recently kept track: in one two-month period last year, I was solicited by more than 100 organizations. Judging from the reports of friends and colleagues, that experience is not unusual. Great causes and energetic fundraisers abound.

Increasingly large sums of money also are involved, in part because our society's tools are changing so dramatically. The $500 school book fund that spun off 5 percent a year used to be sufficient to buy five library books a year, and those books would last (virtually) forever. Today, a library database can cost $10,000, and probably has to be renewed annually. (If you're keeping track, your endowment just had to grow from $500 to $200,000.) Hospitals doing state-of-the-art surgery now depend upon proton knives, which cost as much as $3 million each. This is true in almost every philanthropic realm. Conservation groups, for example, have seen the price per acre of land skyrocket.

As a result, major gifts have become more important to the success of organizations, and major donors are highly sought after. Some of those major donors have responded by becoming more sophisticated in their philanthropic decision-making. Others are just confused, even overwhelmed.

As nonprofit leaders, we wonder: How can we compete? How can we survive and thrive?

One day not long ago, I was having a conversation with Allen Grossman, former president of Outward Bound, about those very questions. The discussion turned to the nature of nonprofits. Allen asserted that the main differences between nonprofits and for-profits stem from the fact that nonprofits' missions almost always exceed their resources. I wasn't about to argue the challenge of responding to social needs, particularly at a time when an economic downturn was dampening philanthropic contributions and spiking demand for services. I *did* argue, though, for another way of looking at it: *nonprofits pursue opportunities beyond the resources they currently control.*

Maybe you won't be surprised to learn that I say exactly the same thing about entrepreneurs. Entrepreneurs see a need, and become convinced that they can meet that need. Then, they make it happen—almost always without controlling the necessary resources at the starting line.

This, I think, is an overlap of enormous importance. I believe that nonprofits must think and act like entrepreneurs, to be able to make significant and positive change in a world that is increasingly in need of their help. Fundraising is the philanthropic income-generation part of a nonprofit's economic model. It's not conducted in a vacuum; it's part of the organization's management systems and its day-to-day work. So don't be surprised, as you read this book, to encounter space devoted to management issues and approaches.

It is no accident that ever-larger numbers of successful entrepreneurs are launching nonprofit ventures. Bill Gates is an oft-cited example. But consider also Avichai (Avi) Kremer, a former officer in the Israeli Defense Force and project manager for a high-tech defense industry firm. Diagnosed with ALS[1] in his first year at HBS, he was stunned, but he vowed to complete his studies. That summer, he returned home to Israel for his already planned internship, and became involved in that country's ALS foundation. He was shocked at how little progress had been made worldwide in finding a cure. ALS,

---

[1] Amyotrophic lateral sclerosis (ALS, also known as Lou Gehrig's disease) is a degenerative disease of nerve cells in the brain and spinal cord that control muscle movement.

he discovered, was not a high priority either for the general public or the pharmaceutical industry.

When he returned to HBS, Avi and a group of his classmates decided to tackle the problem head-on by founding Prize4Life, a nonprofit offering incentive prizes to researchers for solving ALS treatment-related problems. The enterprise has had success in raising both awareness and funds, and sponsoring ALS-dedicated teams in the U.S., Canada, Europe, and the Middle East. Whether you call it social enterprise, social philanthropy, philanthrocapitalism, or any one of the other monikers that have cropped up, it was a compelling case of entrepreneurs jumping in to address a social need.

For me, fundraising is a *personal* thing. It gives me an opportunity to change my world in a positive way. Just as my charitable giving makes visible those values or issues I care about, so do my fundraising activities. This is critically important. As a fundraising leader, *you need to feel a personal commitment* to the cause and the organization that you choose to support and promote. Not only will you be more effective, but you also will derive much greater satisfaction from your work.

Logically, then, the question becomes: *How do you want to change the world?*

ABOUT THIS BOOK

In 2008, coming up on retirement, I was teaching my last MBA course. Shirley Spence, a former partner at Mercer Management Consulting (now Oliver Wyman) was working with me as an HBS research associate. I asked her if she might be interested in collaborating on a book about fundraising. I had decided to share my perspective, and what I have learned about fundraising in general, and what I know best in particular—"significant" fundraising, which is my own terminology for what others call "major gifts." (More on this below.) I wanted to speak to fundraising leaders about the challenges and opportunities they face. I didn't know if anyone would want to read a book about that, but I knew I wanted to write it. Fortunately, Shirley gave me an enthusiastic *yes*.

Since then, we have looked at what's going on in the contemporary world of philanthropy. Yes, we have spent many hours talking about my own fundraising experience. But we've also scrutinized a wide range of institutions and individuals for fundraising do's and don'ts. We solicited input from experienced volunteer and professional fundraisers. We interviewed several philanthropic individuals I know, probing for the donor's perspective. As we reflected on all that, we tried to extract the essence of effective fundraising.

The research process has been illuminating. It has

reinforced our belief in the importance of taking the donor's perspective. We use the term "significant" rather than "major" gift for just this reason. The way I look at it, gift size shouldn't be viewed as an absolute number; it should be considered relative to the donor's financial means, and his or her willingness to "stretch." A significant gift for a young graduate might be $100; for an aging billionaire, that could be $100 million. Again, it's a relative measure.

Asking and answering some critical donor questions—aimed at successfully making your case for a significant gift—has become the core of the book. We have settled on four key questions that a donor must implicitly say "yes" to, about your organization and cause:

- Are you doing important work?
- Are you well managed?
- Will my gift make a difference?
- Will the experience be satisfying to me?

We became satisfied that those questions are pertinent for significant gifts, regardless of the size of the gift, the size of the organization, the cause being championed, or where in the world you might be. Assuming that you can answer them, the reality is that most philanthropists *want to* give.

We also became further convinced of the importance of an entrepreneurial mindset and approach, and of the critical role played by fundraising leadership. Some things can't just happen; they need strong and skilled leadership. A well-run effort can generate positive outcomes for years; a mismanaged fundraising activity can also have consequences—negative!—far into the future.

The structure of this book reflects my and Shirley's journey. As noted, it is organized around our four questions, with some concluding thoughts about being a fundraising leader. Throughout, there are lots of stories. Many of them are mine, but many others come from institutions and individuals providing valuable examples of fundraising leaders—and donors—at work. You will encounter examples ranging from a small conservation project to a multimillion-dollar campaign. You will learn from the experience of educational institutions, hospitals, and social service organizations. You may or may not see an organization that looks exactly like yours. But even if you don't, the examples should help you think more clearly about your own situation, and how you and your cause can do better.

My hope is that this book will help you—whether you are a donor, board member, executive director, or a volunteer who wants to raise money—feel more comfortable in your fundraising role, and better equipped to succeed. I hope it will help you be more effective in working with fundraising professionals and volunteers. I hope it will enable you to better guide donors, and frame their thinking as they make philanthropic decisions. Perhaps it may even help you think about your own giving decisions.

Most of all, I hope to convince you that fundraising offers you a tremendous opportunity to have a positive impact on your world—the people and things you care about—while at the same time having a deeply satisfying experience.

And yes, fundraising is fun.

CHAPTER 1

FUNDRAISING: THE FOUR BIG QUESTIONS

Not long ago, I was giving a talk on fundraising to a group of nonprofit executives. I began by asking for stories about their best and worst fundraising experiences. What worked, and what didn't?

One of the people in the room picked up on this latter question. He reported that while some of his prospects responded to his pitch enthusiastically, others were lukewarm at best. And yet—he continued, displaying a mixture of puzzlement and indignation—he was making *exactly the same pitch* each time! Why were the responses all over the map?

Around the room, many heads were nodding in sympathy. *Why, indeed?*

From the way I've related this story, and from your own experience, you probably already know the answer. A "one size fits all" approach to fundraising can't work consistently, because it fails to take into account the fact that donors come in all shapes and sizes, with their own stories and aspirations. Your job as a fundraiser is to arrive at a deep understanding of what motivates each donor, and consider what you are proposing *from his or her perspective.*

UNDERSTANDING DONOR MOTIVATIONS

I believe that there are four things that make us feel successful in life: achievement, significance, legacy, and happiness. Philanthropy is an opportunity to satisfy each of these key motivations. So in order to make a compelling case that someone should join you in your cause, you'll want to *tap into one or more of those four components of lasting success.*

First, some background. Research that a colleague and I conducted some years ago showed that enduring success has those same four central dimensions. (See **Figure 1-1**) The single-minded pursuit of only one of these elements isn't enough; you have to attain "just enough" of each to achieve success. And just to complicate the equation, our research showed that it's not good enough to touch these bases sequentially (e.g., "have fun now; give back later"). It turns out that you have to touch each of the four bases with some regularity, over the course of your lifetime.[2]

FIGURE 1-1: COMPONENTS OF LASTING SUCCESS

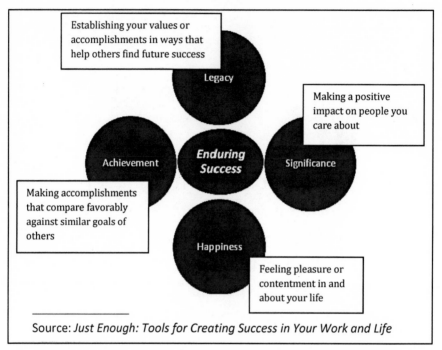

Source: *Just Enough: Tools for Creating Success in Your Work and Life*

What does this have to do with fundraising? You may find it a useful way to think about the satisfactions inherent in giving, and about what might motivate someone to give to your organization or cause. Let's look briefly at each of these four touchstones.

For some people, *achievement* means being recognized by their peers. They want to be part of "the group," and are motivated to give in order to gain social access or

---

[2] Nash, Laura and Howard Stevenson. *Just Enough: Tools for Creating Success in Your Work and Life*. Hoboken NJ: John Wiley & Sons, 2004.

acceptance. They may donate to an arts organization in anticipation of being invited to the "right" parties. They may contribute to a foundation that supports their particular profession or expertise, in hopes of getting recognition within that group.

Others respond to an opportunity so that they can be of *significance,* in many cases by helping address an urgent need. Dire circumstances brought on by some sort of catastrophe, in particular can motivate people to step up. Partners in Health—a highly regarded organization providing community-based health care to some of the poorest areas in the world—offers a compelling example. After the devastating earthquake in Haiti in 2010, the Partners in Health donor base exploded from 6,000 to 81,000, almost overwhelming its systems.

The desire to do something on this earth that will matter when you're gone—to have a major and lasting impact—is a powerful motivator for some. *Legacy* giving can be with or without acclaim, before or after death. In 2009, one donor caused quite a stir by making multimillion-dollar gifts to several universities, and by doing so anonymously. Legacy giving isn't necessarily about *public* recognition, or success in the near term. A bequest will not give you fame in your lifetime, and the impact of a significant gift towards finding a cure for a deadly disease, or addressing an environmental threat, may well not be seen or felt for decades.

Last, but far from least, there is *happiness*. Some individuals will write a check just to escape the fundraiser. And it has become the fashion, in some circles, to offer opportunities to contribute to avoid having to attend a fundraising gala. But especially when a significant gift is involved, most donors just plain feel good when they give. You've given back; you've done your share; you've made the world a better place. What a friend of mine calls payback, and others may call gratitude, can be a factor. Sidney Knafel, who donated $20 million to build a center for government and international relations at Harvard University, put it this way: *"Don't give until it hurts. Give until it feels good."*

These four motivations are not mutually exclusive, of course. In some situations, all are operating together. In others, one will be predominant. For still others, they may differ depending on the giving opportunity in question or the point in time. For most donors, achievement will tend to be dominant when young, and legacy when older. But whether your prospect is young or old, you need to understand when that prospect might be thinking about making a significant gift. Planned life transitions (such as retirement and significant financial transactions) can serve as one kind of trigger; unplanned events (for example, illness) can serve as another.

When I became involved in HBS fundraising, I couldn't understand why 25th reunion-goers were considered prime giving targets. One day the answer occurred to me: in that traditional mindset, that was about the age when college graduates were expected to come into their inheritances. Times have changed! Today, it's more about entrepreneurs making their own way, which means that most large gifts come later in life. It also means that you have to start wooing them early, for smaller gifts, since everyone will be targeting those entrepreneurs when their dreams pan out, and their success becomes widely known.

I used the donor-motivation framework at NPR to encourage donor-centered thinking when we were embarking on a new fundraising strategy. Traditionally, we relied on programming fees from stations and corporate sponsorships for the bulk of our revenues. When a dismal economic environment caused a serious drop in corporate sponsorships, we decided to launch a major gifts campaign.

These were unfamiliar waters, so I asked NPR staff members: what would appeal to an NPR donor looking for a sense of *achievement*? Several answers emerged. Some people got a lot of satisfaction from an on-air mention during phone-a-thons. (They felt that they had "arrived.") Others felt a sense of accomplishment from what they learned by listening to NPR. Still others were drawn by the opportunity to lead a fundraising team, or serve on the board. Clearly, "achievement" could mean different things to different people.

What about the other three potential satisfactions inherent in giving? For some, it seemed, *significance* grew out of a sense of noblesse oblige—the obligation of a privileged person to fix something that most people lacked the means to fix. For example: if newspapers were truly dying, and if the only alternatives were partisan outlets (e.g., FoxNews, MSNBC) presenting overheated opinions disguised as news, then these donors felt obligated to provide intellectually honest news and non-commercial cultural content to the nation, and thereby support an informed public debate.

Happiness? For some, it was about their personal enjoyment of the content, and the feeling of being "among friends" in the virtual community of the airwaves. Tuning in to NPR while making the morning coffee or driving to work was a familiar, even comforting part of many people's daily routine, and for those people, "Guess what I heard on NPR!" served as a great conversation-starter. At NPR, we talk about "driveway moments," when a listener is so engrossed that he will stay in the car just to hear the end of the story. For many of these people, significantly, learning was not particularly important, and *applying* that learning was even less important. Lots of people loved *Car Talk*; almost none of them had any intention of rebuilding their engines.

For people seeking the satisfaction of *legacy*, NPR offered an opportunity to sustain a type of information and cultural experience that they valued, and felt others should be exposed to. This was somewhat different from "significance," in that legacy-oriented donors hoped to have an impact long after they were gone. For example: one donor had earmarked a large gift for NPR's *Planet Money* program because he felt economic literacy was important, both for current and future generations. Others gave to support the institution as a whole, and to ensure the continuation of its mission. Also of note: the Newseum in Washington, D.C., celebrates freedom of the press, and is supported by many who believe that this is a fundamental underpinning of our society.

During our discussions, the subject of "giveaways" came up. Some people felt that the free NPR umbrella offered during phone-a-thons had great appeal as a tangible "get" for donors: *Make a contribution; get a good umbrella*. I argued for a less transactional way of looking at it. My idea was to put an NPR hat or T-shirt on each person's seat at a Weekend in Washington event for donors at the $5,000-and-over level. My NPR colleagues were a tad skeptical: donors at this level obviously didn't need clothes. How excited would they be about getting a hat, or a T-shirt? We did it anyway. By one eyeball estimate (mine), something more than 40 percent of our guests immediately put them on. It was a way for them to identify with the organization, and the group. Feeling "part of it" was the real reward. That approach—giving people things that they can afford, don't really need, but love to receive—has continued.

Overall, I wound up pleased with the results of the NPR exercise. It produced some good ideas, and built a sense of teamwork and momentum. Perhaps most important, it helped the NPR staff begin to think more *from the perspective of the donor*, as we went about the business of fundraising.

Copyright Grantland Enterprises; www.grantland.net

THE FOUR BIG QUESTIONS

As a fundraiser who believes strongly in a particular cause, you are trying to do two things: 1) find like-minded individuals, and 2) convince them that your organization is uniquely positioned (or at least extremely well positioned) to address a problem that they deeply care about. Let's face it: they have many places to invest their dollars, and maybe even other places that do something like what you do. So why should they give to *your* organization, and to the particular giving opportunity you may be proposing?

Let's dig deeper into the potential donor's psychology by exploring the four key questions that he or she is likely to have in mind. These four questions, introduced earlier in this book and summarized in **Figure 1-2**, are about both the *organization* and the *gift*. You should expect to have to address all of them during the process of soliciting a gift. In fact, they form the basis for most of my gift proposals.

FIGURE 1-2: THE DONOR'S FOUR QUESTIONS

1. Are you doing important work? 2. Are you well managed?	*About the organization*
3. Will my gift make a difference? 4. Will the experience be satisfying to me?	*About the giving*

The first and most important question is: *Are you doing important work?* And, of course, what they mean by that question is: Are you doing *what I consider* to be important work? If your mission holds no interest for them, don't waste your time trying to convince them. But let's assume that they're interested, even enthused. They're still not about to toss their money into a black hole. Most people, unfortunately, have heard stories about the mismanagement of funds by a nonprofit; some have even seen it firsthand. So the next question you should anticipate is: *Are you well managed?*

If you can get over that hurdle, your organization has passed the litmus test, and attention will turn to how the money will be used: *Will my gift make a difference?* In my experience, most people who give a significant gift are truly interested in making an impact for positive change. They want reassurance not only that their money won't be wasted, but that it will be used effectively. And, finally: *Will the experience be satisfying to me?* This is a key principle of this book: you start answering this question from the moment you first start working with a donor to the receipt of the gift—and far beyond, in many cases.

NPR's experience with Joan Kroc, wife of the founder of McDonald's Corporation, is instructive. Ray Kroc died in 1984, leaving her his fortune and his ownership position in the San Diego Padres. For Joan, the latter legacy presented interesting opportunities. As an owner, she started Major League Baseball's first employee-assistance program for players and staff with drug problems. After a failed attempt to donate the team to the city of San Diego, she sold it and turned her attention to philanthropy, giving generously to support causes in the San Diego area, including an $18.5 million gift for a hospice center and an $87 million gift for a Salvation Army community center. She became personally involved in the Grand Forks, North Dakota, and East Grand Forks, Minnesota communities that were devastated by a flood in 1987, donating $15 million and helping out in person at homeless shelters. She also was generous in supporting peace studies and nuclear disarmament. As a rule, Joan preferred to give anonymously, but recipients of her generosity often insisted on generating publicity around the gifts, in hopes of creating a buzz and attracting additional donors. She understood and tolerated those efforts, but for her, "legacy" was not about public recognition.

Joan was a staunch supporter of an informed civic society, and believed in the power of public radio. She herself had enjoyed NPR programming over the years. As she began to plan her bequests, she approached NPR regarding a gift. NPR executives were startled—and understandably delighted—and immediately flew to San Diego to meet with her. Joan quickly made it clear, though, that she would insist on an extensive due-diligence process before she would make a sizeable commitment to the organization. NPR would have to withstand the scrutiny of her professional staff. Was the organization well managed? How could it guarantee that Joan's bequest would be used in accordance with her wishes, in perpetuity?

NPR evidently cleared these hurdles. When Joan died in 2003, her will specified substantial gifts to a number of familiar institutions, including an astounding $1.6 billion contribution to the Salvation Army. But there were several new beneficiaries, as well. NPR received more than $200 million, and an additional $5 million went to a member station in San Diego. Interestingly enough, NPR executives heard later that Joan had initially approached another public media group, but had been off put by its lack of responsiveness. If that was true, that other organization made a $200 million mistake.

Why public radio? It's clear that Joan was motivated by the value of the programming to her personally, and her desire to have a lasting impact on her neighbors and society in general. But as a sophisticated philanthropist, she knew she had options. All four of the questions outlined above had to be answered to her satisfaction before she would make a gift.

Every now and then, you may stumble upon a donor who is so passionate about your cause that he or she is ready to write a check on the spot. Great—but I wouldn't advise counting on that happy outcome! And, yes, there are those who are largely disinterested in the first three questions. They may just want the satisfaction of having their friends and colleagues see their name on a list, or a plaque in a lobby.

That's not the norm either—although I certainly wouldn't turn the money down, assuming it tracks with the best interests of your institution and its work.

And yes, there are unsophisticated donors out there who don't know about how to go about philanthropy, and need some education and guidance. I recently spent quite a lot of time with an individual who wanted to donate $1 million to "something." I spent time helping him sort through his options, which of course included some causes close to my own heart. A generous donor, who also is a highly effective fundraiser, made this observation:

I believe that philanthropy is a learned thing. I've found that there are many more people with resources looking for meaning, than people with meaning looking for resources. As a nonprofit, you create meaning by raising money.

But these are all exceptions to my cardinal rule, which is, *Be prepared to answer all four questions,* even in cases where they're not all explicitly posed. Why? Because considered from the donor's perspective, they combine to tell a compelling story. So you have to ask them of your organization, and make sure you personally are satisfied with the answers. If you aren't, you have a problem. *You* have to be convinced, before you can hope to convince anyone else.

THE "SECRET" FORMULA

If you think about it, there's a simple formula that underlies all fundraising, both good and bad. It's summarized in **Figure 1-3**:

FIGURE **1-3**: FUNDRAISING FORMULA AND LEVERS

Number of donors	X	Closing %	X	Average gift	=	Total dollars

How do we get more donors?
- Have a clear message
- Carefully cast your net
- Get out and ask

How do we get more "yes-es?"?
- Target donor's interests
- Appeal to the head and the heart
- Get the timing right

How do we incite a larger gift?
- Understand resources available
- Ask for a *significant* gift
- Build over time

It's hardly a "secret" formula; just plain algebra, really. But maybe you haven't thought about it in exactly these terms before. Assume a blank slate. Simply stated, if you multiply number of donors by closing percentage and average gift size, you arrive at a total-dollars-raised estimate. But as the columns in Figure 1-3 make clear, *each of the variables in the formula is actually a point of leverage.*

Take the third column, having to do with larger gifts. One thing I've noticed over the years is that organizations tend to underestimate their donors. I believe in aiming high, while still being realistic. For example, the conservation group in the area where I have a summer home wanted to raise $500,000 to protect threatened marshlands. The director's plan was to solicit 100 donations of $5,000 each. Knowing the community and its means, I suggested getting one donation of $100,000, and two of $50,000, to set a giving norm, and then going to neighbors with that information. I call that "getting the bell cow"—in other words, finding someone to lead the herd. The strategy worked: the campaign was completed in less than two weeks, to the surprise and delight of the director. Many small gifts followed, but the hard work was done.

All too often, we get trapped in the status quo, and assume that the way things are is the way things have to be. In most cases, that's not true. At Sudbury Valley Trustees, it took an enormous effort for me to convince the board to raise membership fees from $35 to $50. When we did, no one blinked. The same was true for public radio memberships.

Part of the power and value of this approach lies in its implications for both fundraising *effectiveness* and *efficiency*. For example, if you increase your average gift and/or improve your closing rate, you can reduce the number of donors needed, and still hit your fundraising goal. Because you are dealing with fewer donors, you will need fewer staff for all the behind-the-scenes work, and you can lighten the load on your volunteers.

By improving on any of these measures, you can positively affect your total dollars raised. And you can get better, as you go. You can use the formula to test actionable options, based on the best available information at any point in time—i.e., making educated guesses to start, and introducing refinements as you go along.

How does this tie into the four questions? Successfully addressing the four questions can improve your results on each fundraising variable, by helping target the best prospects, identifying opportunities that are giving priorities, and making a case that appeals to the head and the heart. At this point, I'd add another variable: time. Well done, fundraising from the donor perspective should yield a mutually satisfying relationship that sets the stage for further giving.

Copyright Grantland Enterprises; www. grantland.net

INDIVIDUAL FUNDRAISING STRATEGIES – SOME OPTIONS

Of course, the fundraising formula is just part of the work of developing a strategy for individual fundraising. There are many different fundraising strategies, four of which are pictured in **Figure 1-4**, and summarized below.

FIGURE 1-4: FOUR BASIC STRATEGIC OPTIONS

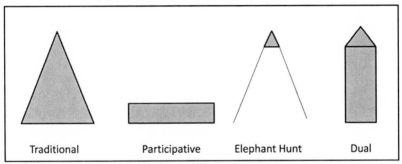

| Traditional | Participative | Elephant Hunt | Dual |

The Traditional Pyramid Strategy

No doubt you've heard the phrase "gift pyramid" (or "pyramid of giving"). The pyramid reflects wealth distribution, and assumes giving at all levels, with 80 to 90 percent of all funds received coming from the top of the pyramid. It is the outcome of what could be described as a funnel strategy: pour a lot in, and a few good ones will come out. This is the dominant strategy at many universities, in part because they start with a relatively large and identifiable donor pool. (It's also common among annual funds.) One goal of the pyramid strategy is to create a "habit of giving," in hopes that people will ratchet up their contributions over time.

I have no issue with gift pyramids per se, just with their single-minded use. There is nothing in the world that says that is how fundraising should work. Pyramids reflect just one strategy for fundraising. The challenge is to determine which option is best for your situation. If you do use a pyramid, its shape should reflect your fundraising strategy (and not the other way around!); it's an outcome, not a method.

The Participative Strategy

In this model, you want everyone to give at least something. "From each according to his means," is the mantra. This can be important for credibility, which is why 100 percent participation from board members is essential. It also can be important for rallying an entire organization behind a cause.

The Elephant Hunt Strategy

Some causes and organizations don't have a broad appeal, so there is little point to looking at the bottom of the pyramid. Their supporters are few, but passionate. An astronomical lab seeking funding for a cutting-edge ("very expensive") telescope has no choice but to use this approach. Health-care philanthropy (e.g., a new cancer wing or cardiovascular center) also tends to embrace this model.

The Dual Strategy

A dual strategy uses two different strategies for two different purposes. It's a common approach in membership organizations where the goal is to maximize ongoing participation, and go elephant hunting for funders of large projects. It will require telling the same story differently, for the different target groups.

THE LAST WORD, FROM A DONOR

In this chapter, we've explored motivations, raised key questions, invoked formulas, and introduced strategies. All are important, but I want to single out and underscore a core theme of this chapter: *the importance of the donor perspective.*

Toward that end, I'll give the last word to one of the donors interviewed for this book, Joe O'Donnell, who also happens to be one of the best fundraisers I know.

A PHILANTHROPIST'S STORY – JOE O'DONNELL

Born in 1944, Joe grew up in a blue-collar neighborhood in Everett, MA. His father, a policeman, and mother, a homemaker, were strong believers in the value of education. Joe attended parochial elementary and high school, and when the time came for college, Joe found himself courted by a number of schools for his football prowess. He also applied to Harvard—not exactly a football powerhouse—and vividly recalled having an interview there, with his father in the room:

> At the end of the interview, Fred Glimp, the admissions officer turned to my dad and said: "He's a great kid. If he were my son, I'd send him to Exeter for a year." I was shocked, but my father took his advice to heart. Within a month, I was enrolled at Exeter with a full scholarship. It turned out to be the perfect transition to Harvard, and I'll never forget that someone was smart enough to see that I needed that. I started Harvard the next year, again with a scholarship, and fully prepared.

After graduation, Joe attended HBS. While there, he had the idea for starting a service to help students find off-campus housing. The dean agreed, and he launched what proved to be a successful venture. During his second year at HBS, he received a job offer from Ross Perot at EDS. He was tempted by the prestige and money, but—with the help of his new wife—realized it would be a poor fit for someone with an entrepreneurial bent. He ended up being hired by the HBS dean, and more or less running the administrative side of the school.

Life changed dramatically when Joe's son, Joey, was born with cystic fibrosis. Faced with huge medical bills, Joe realized he needed to make more money. His goal was to join a small, service-oriented company

A PHILANTHROPIST'S STORY – JOE O'DONNELL (CONT.)

with entrepreneurial potential and room to grow. "Wherever I went," he recalls, "I wanted to have an impact." He landed a job with a concession company that he ended up buying, and built it into a privately held, billion-dollar leisure and recreation business called "Boston Culinary Group." In 2005, one magazine ranked him the most powerful man in Boston.

Joe expressed his gratitude for his educational opportunities by supporting Exeter, Harvard, and HBS. He was active in school governance, a generous donor, and an energetic fundraiser. For his 25th HBS reunion, for example, Joe and a handful of classmates decided to take a more targeted approach than usual to fundraising, crisscrossing the country to personally solicit from selected prospects. The result, as Joe recalls it: "We got eight $1 million gifts, and filled in around that to get to $15 million. The most any class had raised before that was $7 million, and the average class gift was $4 million"

The cause closest to Joe's heart, however, was cystic fibrosis. During his son's treatment, Joe and his wife were involved in a foundation that supported families with the disease. Joey's death at age 12 was a personal tragedy, and also prompted Joe to reflect on "giving back." He explained:

What my wife and I learned from spending years in the hospital was that there are lots of important things in life, but until they are shoved right in your face, you might not see how important those things are. None of us will live forever, and as far as I know, none of us has figured out how to take our riches with us. Our time here is short, and you have to ask yourself what you're going to do with your money.

A PHILANTHROPIST'S STORY – JOE O'DONNELL (CONT.)

Part of my wanting to give back also came from a 75-year-old friend. I said to him: "You've been the most successful person I know. If you could go back, what would you do differently?" He said: "I'd start giving my money away, and doing good things earlier. It was ridiculous. I have all this money, and my kids have more money than they need, so I should have started earlier." He was a very philanthropic person, but had only started giving back at age 65. That was a huge "aha," for me.

Joe and his family went on to found the Joey Fund, and become ardent supporters of activities related to cystic fibrosis. The Cystic Fibrosis Foundation raises $165 million a year from fundraising events organized by 75 chapters and branch offices, and is proud to be ranked one of the most efficient organizations of its kind. Joe and his family are involved in other causes as well, with Joe spending almost half his time on philanthropic activities, in addition to his responsibilities as chairman and CEO of Boston Culinary. He commented:

Giving back has been a major part of our life. Our two daughters are very aware of our thinking on this. We're trying to raise them within a framework of knowing that they're very fortunate and other people aren't, so it's our responsibility to help. I was pleasantly surprised to learn that one of them was doing her senior thesis at Harvard on venture philanthropy.

CHAPTER 2

ARE YOU DOING IMPORTANT WORK?

When I first meet with a prospect, I often begin by saying something to the effect of, "I'm asking you to share in something I believe is important."

There are two reasons why I open on that note. First, as a volunteer, I can speak this way with more passion and credibility than a professional, because I have no financial motivation. I'm a *peer*, more or less, of the person with whom I'm talking. Second, fundraising isn't a one-way endeavor; it's about making a match between individuals and institutions that have a shared vision. Successful fundraising creates a partnership where both parties contribute to changing the world.

This presumes the organization that is seeking funds has clearly defined its mission—but of course, that's not always the case. (Even organizations with a seemingly clear profile often have trouble articulating the "elevator message," the succinct and compelling explanation that could be delivered between floors 1 and 10.) Unfortunately, this work can be trumped by other day-today challenges, and the necessary definitional work may not get done.

We at NPR weren't immune to the fuzzy-mission syndrome. The issue came to a head as we began preparing for a major gift campaign. One day a staff member approached me, and—with obvious pride—presented me with the fruits of her labors over the previous several weeks. It turned out to be a list of wealthy people.

Copyright Grantland Enterprises; www.grantland.net

I didn't want to discourage her, but I felt she had to hear the truth. "Finding rich people is not the problem," I told her. "I know a hundred of them, maybe more. Or we can just go out and get a Forbes list." In fact, there are plenty of good sources of information about rich people.

"Our *real* problem," I continued, "is knowing what we're selling. Once we know that, we can start looking for the people who might be interested."

That's the focus of this chapter.

MISSION, MESSAGE, AND MONEY

How are mission, message, and money interrelated? Let's consider a storied and somewhat controversial example: the March of Dimes Foundation. Established in 1938 by President Roosevelt, the March of Dimes was conceived as a partnership between scientists and volunteers to battle polio. Its name was coined by an entertainer who—promoting the organization's first fundraiser—asked people to send dimes to the White House.

A massive fundraising infrastructure was created, which helped pay for the development and field trials of the Salk vaccine. By 1955, the foundation had accomplished its goal; the vaccine was proven safe and effective. What now? It had a powerful brand name and nationwide network of researchers, volunteers, educators, outreach workers, and advocates. Would it close its doors, or redirect its efforts? After considerable debate, it adopted a charter of broader medical causes, and in 1958 renamed itself the "National Foundation." Perhaps not surprisingly, charitable contributions began to plummet.

In 1965, the foundation's leadership announced that it would focus exclusively on birth defects. Fundraising improved, and a new name emerged: the "March of Dimes Birth Defects Foundation." Impressive advances were made in research, treatment, education, and legislation. In the early 2000s, however, the March of

Dimes experienced several years of declines in fundraising. Leadership paused for self-examination, commissioned Gallup polls and focus groups, and concluded that it wasn't "doing a good enough job of getting the word out."[3] As a result, the focus was shifted from "birth defects" to "healthy babies." It dropped "birth defects" from its name, and its mission became to improve the health of babies by preventing premature birth and infant mortality, as well as birth defects. The more upbeat message seemed to have a positive effect on fundraising, and today the foundation presses on with its work.

This is not exactly a classic example of a mission-driven organization. Rather, it's a case of an institution looking for a way to leverage its ability to do good, over the long term. I think that's fine—so long as the organization remains focused on pursuing opportunities to fill an important social need. The key lesson is the tight interplay of mission, message, and money.

Now, let's refocus on you. Here's a quick quiz. Think about the nonprofit institution you're involved with, and ask yourself—and perhaps others in your organization— the following questions:

---

[3] "March of Dimes Second Act," William P. Barrett, Forbes, 11/19/2008 (www.forbes.com)

- Does our organization have a shared understanding of the work we do and why it's important? Are we clear about what we *don't* do?
- Am I—and is the rest of the organization— committed to, and even passionate about, our mission? Who else will care about this mission?
- Can we articulate our mission in a clear and compelling way to donors and other stakeholders?

If you answered "yes" to all three, I applaud you and your organization. If you didn't, here are some good questions to ponder:

- What is our service model? Whom will we serve? What services will we offer? What processes will we perform?
- How will we achieve this? What are our distinctive competencies?
- What do we stand for? What are our core values?
- Who are our stakeholders? What are our commitments to them?
- What are our goals? What outcomes will we achieve?
- What are our performance standards? How will we measure them?

Once those questions are answered, you need to articulate what you're all about in a way that is memorable, differentiable, credible, inspirational, and aspirational. And I can't say it too often, or too forcefully: keep it *simple*. Here's an interesting test: is it something that people could sing? (It's easier to sing Rodgers and Hammerstein than Andrew Lloyd Webber.)

Your mission is often the first thing that people see or hear about you. Trust me; the words matter. During NPR discussions of our mission statement, the phrase "challenging your thinking" landed on the table. Many of us (including me) thought that sounded too confrontational and partisan. Another choice, "informing in the context of a rapidly changing world," seemed to resonate better, suggesting that NPR would help audiences make sense of things.

You and everyone else in your organization should be able to articulate your mission—with clarity and, ideally, passion. Below is a sampling of nonprofit mission statements. Some are better than others. Use the following criteria—*memorable, differentiable, credible, inspirational, aspirational,* and *simple*—to decide how effective you think each is.

NONPROFIT MISSION STATEMENTS: SOME EXAMPLES

Doctors Without Borders

[We] deliver emergency medical assistance to people affected by armed conflict, epidemics, malnutrition, natural disasters, or exclusion from health care in nearly 60 countries. An interdependent international humanitarian organization, [DWB] unites direct medical care with a commitment to bearing witness to the plight of the people it assists.

Rosie's Place (Boston)

[Our] mission is to provide a safe and nurturing environment for poor and homeless women to maintain their dignity, seek opportunity and find security in their lives.

Arts Learning

[Our] mission is to encourage the active engagement of preschool through college students in developing their highest artistic and academic competence.

Nature Conservancy

[Our] mission is to preserve the plants, animals and natural communities that represent the diversity of life on earth by protecting the lands and waters they need to survive.

Los Angeles Unified School District

[Our] teachers, administrators and staff believe in the equal worth and dignity of all students and are committed to educate all students to their maximum potential.

Toronto (Canada) District School Board

Our mission is to enable all students to reach high levels of achievement and acquire knowledge, skills and values they need to

NONPROFIT MISSION STATEMENTS: SOME EXAMPLES (CONT.)
become responsible members of a democratic society.

University of Texas MD Anderson Cancer
[Our] mission is to eliminate cancer in Texas, the nation, and the world through outstanding programs that integrate patient care, research and prevention, and through education for undergraduate and graduate students, trainees, professionals, employees and the public.

Winchester Hospital (Winchester MA)
To care. To heal. To excel. In service to our community.

INSEAD (international business school)
Our mission is to promote a non-dogmatic learning environment that brings together people, cultures and ideas from around the world, changing lives, and helping transform organizations through management education.

San Francisco Ballet
The mission of San Francisco Ballet is to share the joy of dance with its community and around the globe and to provide the highest caliber of dance training in its School. San Francisco Ballet seeks to enhance its position as one of the world's finest dance companies through its vitality, innovation, and diversity and through its uncompromising commitment to artistic excellence based in the classical ballet tradition.

As you develop your mission, be both *bold* and *realistic*. (The right scale of effort is critical, for credibility as well as impact.) Your scope and focus will follow from your mission. This point is illustrated by a land conservation group whose mission at one time was to "preserve open space," a goal that it had traditionally measured in terms of raw acres preserved. Over time, it found itself buying more and more open space in rural Arizona—in other words, inexpensive acreage that helped "run up the numbers." Unfortunately, that cheap land was neither in danger of being developed nor ecologically important. When the nonprofit seriously looked at why it wanted to preserve open space, it realized that its *real* goal was to save ecologically significant habitats. That realization led to a much more meaningful and impactful mission—and, not surprisingly, a much more compelling pitch to funders.

One cautionary tale related to mission involves a music conservatory. Traditionally, its mission focused on "developing world-class musicians." The problem was that the school had "only" a 1 percent success rate. Why? The answer is complicated, but success as a professional musician is usually a function of far more than just talent and training; a lucky break (or someone else's unlucky break) is often the decisive factor. So even though "one in a hundred" was actually an *outstanding* track record, the parents of the students—a primary target—weren't giving. With the best of intentions, the conservatory was creating false expectations (a career as a world-class musician!), and then failing to achieve that nearly unattainable goal, and thereby scaring off donors.

What the school *could* realistically offer was the discipline of rigorous training, a love of music that would last a lifetime, and (of course) a special push to those good enough to move on and compete on the musical fast track. With this restatement of mission, several key leaders agreed, the school would be better able to build bridges to its prospective donors. But it didn't happen. I am sorry to report that the old mission lives on—tradition dies hard!—and the conservatory still has a tough time raising the needed funds.

Sometimes, a big-picture approach is needed to tackle the question of scope and focus. An effort called "BioMap2" offers an interesting example. Four organizations with similar missions, goals, and science-based approaches—the Massachusetts Department of Fish and Game, the Division of Fisheries and Wildlife, the Natural Heritage & Endangered Species Program, and the Nature Conservancy—pooled their data and expertise to identify critical habitats and ecosystems, and create an ambitious but realistic blueprint for conserving the biodiversity of Massachusetts in the face of climate change and other threats. That framework guides the missions and work of many small conservation groups, resulting in a coordinated and collaborative effort.[4] Again, this is the kind of coherent and cohesive thinking that appeals to donors.

What do these stories tell us? They show clearly that the value of a mission statement extends far beyond fundraising. Your mission statement—or vision, or purpose, or whatever you choose to call it—is an organizational linchpin. The process of defining a mission for your organization can be powerful and unifying, yielding clarity and consensus on what you are all about. It defines your desired end state, and can be used to facilitate trade-offs and prioritization, guide day-to-day decisions and resource allocation, foster accountability, and shape culture. What it excludes—that which you *don't* do—is as important as what it includes.

Focusing intensively on mission can help you avoid two common mistakes. The first is accepting funding for projects that aren't consistent with your mission, which can cause you to veer off course, and end up with a jumble of unrelated initiatives driven by donors' wishes rather than what you set out to accomplish. The second is making the institution, rather than the cause it serves,

---

[4] *BioMap2: Conserving the Biodiversity of Massachusetts in a Changing World* report, Commonwealth of Massachusetts –DFG and The Nature Conservancy, 2010.

your priority. Focusing on the institution tends to lead to the creation of a laundry list of things that the institution thinks it needs to function effectively. Such a list—or at least some of the items on it—may be of interest to some donors. But it will almost certainly turn off potential significant supporters who could have been inspired by your broader purpose.

So at the risk of raising a few eyebrows, I'll go so far as to say *mission first, then donors*. Yes, donors provide the lifeblood of many nonprofits, and acquiring and retaining donors is the core work of fundraising. But there are compelling reasons why your focus must remain first and foremost on your mission. Some relate to prospect targeting. As I was trying to explain to my NPR colleagues, being mission-driven allows for more selectivity.

Being mission-driven also keeps you from ignoring potential supporters who should not necessarily be dismissed out of hand. One of my favorite philanthropy-related articles is titled, "*An Episcopalian, an Atheist, and a Jew Walk into a Catholic School...*"[5] The article describes a number of non-Catholic "patron saints" who stepped up in big way to support inner-city Catholic schools, because they cared about the kids in those schools, and

_____

[5] "*An Episcopalian, an Atheist, and a Jew Walk into a Catholic School...*", Christopher Levenick, Philanthropy Roundtable, April 1, 2010

saw the parochial-school system as performing better and at lower cost than its public counterpart.

IMPORTANT *TO ME*

The other side of the equation, of course, is the individuals you hope will share in your endeavor. How do you find them? As a rule, the best starting point is to enlist natural allies—"believers" in your cause, volunteers involved in your organization, and people who have given before—and then use them to recruit others. One caution about leveraging relationships: Don't just sit around the table picking the brains of your board members, which most likely will yield only a list of the usual suspects.

A second caution that I'll add parenthetically: think hard about whether it's a good idea for you to share your lists with other nonprofits. It's O.K. to share lists, but do it selectively. I know how I got on the lists of a number of organizations that were totally unfamiliar (and uninteresting) to me, and I'm not happy about it. But I don't at all mind being solicited by new land conservation groups.

Obviously, you have to do your homework, too. (Note again, though—as I emphasized at the beginning of this chapter—that this homework will be far more productive when it is informed and directed by your mission!) Your staff can draw on databases to develop profiles of potential prospects, including their board involvements, giving histories, financial circumstances, and even their personal interests. There are many such databases available, including (for example) Guidestar, Wealth Trackers, Forbes, Institutional Investor, and Rich Register. Staff support also is invaluable preparing for and following up on donor meetings, and in building and maintaining a robust "homegrown" database on your prospects and your organization's interactions with them. If you don't yet have effective customer-management software in place, consider investing in it; it will make all of this work much easier.

Copyright Grantland Enterprises; www.grantland.net

Building a relationship with your prospects most likely will require a series of one-one meetings, perhaps over an extended period of time. This represents a huge investment of your valuable time. One way of making that investment more productive is to run some sort of preliminary screening. For example: you can invite a select group of individuals to speeches or other events spotlighting the most talented and exciting individuals who are engaged in your cause. Of course, you can't be sure until they show up which prospects will be interested, but those who *do* show up are a self-selected— and promising—group.

When I was helping Harvard University raise money, I arranged for Dr. David Scadden—co-director of the Harvard Stem Cell Institute (HSCI), and co-chair of the University's Stem Cell and Regenerative Biology Department—to give a talk to a group of invited guests about current research on DNA in mental illness. Preliminary findings, as Scadden told the group, suggested strongly that depression has a genetic component. After the presentation, a number of people approached us and told us that depression had been an issue in their families over multiple generations. That gave us an opportunity to follow up with them, to let David drill down on specifics of the research, and—ultimately—to make the case for supporting HSCI 's work.

Another example comes from a Spring Gala that my wife Fredi and I hosted for SummerSearch. Many of the students who had benefited from the program participated in the festivities, and a large number of potential donors were on the guest list. Towards the end of the evening, a friend approached us and said, "You may know that my husband went to Harvard. What you probably *don't* know is that my father was there, too—as a janitor." (In fact, we didn't know that about her.) She herself had gone on to college, and is now a player in the local philanthropic community. Nevertheless, she identified with the SummerSearch students, who were overcoming long odds to make something of themselves. She was—as she put it, with obvious passion and pride—"one of them." She became a loyal and generous supporter.

Once a reasonable list of prospects is assembled, and once you've gotten in the door with a potential donor—often the hardest part of the whole process!—you will need to think on your feet. What makes this person tick? What story can I tell her that will both interest her and help her understand what this organization is all about? What are the grounds for potential collaboration?

Here's a good starting point, taught to me by a great fundraiser: *thank her first for her interest*. It's true—you *do* appreciate her willingness to let you in the door and talk about the subject at hand—and there's no reason not to say so, at the outset.

One thing I try to determine early on is, *Is this a person I can read easily, or will it be a poker game?* A big part of the value of individual meetings is the opportunity to "read" body language and facial expressions, and hear tone of voice. If a poker game it has to be, better to be aware of that fact upfront. In such cases, you may find it helpful to have someone with you at the meeting, watching for subtle indicators of the prospect's reactions or intentions.

In educating your prospects about your organization and its mission, make sure to do it *from their perspective*. The core message is: "We do things you care about. Together, we can accomplish something important and special to you." You are not misrepresenting your organization. You are simply highlighting those aspects of your work that are aligned with their interests. And be sure to use *their* language. Language is about sense making, about how someone thinks about the world. With an MBA, I talk about numbers; with a conservationist, I talk about vernal pools. If someone's politics tend to the right, I may talk about our duty to help the poor; with someone in the liberal camp, I'll phrase it as achieving the goals of equal opportunity.

When it comes down to the central question—*Do we have anything he's interested in?*—I probe for possible matches by using a series of increasingly abstract questions.[6] The basic idea is to start with something concrete ("What are you doing, in general and philanthropically?"), and go step-by-step to a deeper level ("Why are you doing that?"). I'm trying to get at what

---

[6] This is my adaptation of the "five why's"—the problem-solving technique originated by Sakichi Toyoda, incorporated into the Toyota Production System, and subsequently incorporated into part of Kaizen, lean manufacturing, and Six Sigma methodologies.

fundamental problem or problems the prospect is trying to solve through his work and his philanthropy. Then I go backwards from that understanding to see if our institution can offer a realistic solution to that problem.

If you use this approach effectively, you can usually avoid making false assumptions about someone's motivations for giving. This is a trap that's surprisingly easy to fall into. Let's say you have a prospect for your local conservation group. Why might he be interested in something you are doing? He might be concerned about global warming. He might believe that conservation is important to the local ecosystem. He might be looking for a way to be part of a community-based project. He might want nothing more than to protect the view from his house. All very different motivations—and if you guess wrong, you could "lose a sale."

By the way, did you catch that sales analogy? A friend of mine said that he was struck, when reading this book, by the similarities between fundraising and selling. He is quite right, with an important caveat. The approach I take is sometimes described as "Socratic selling" which is quite different from – and more effective than - "hard" sales techniques. (If you're interested, it might be worth checking out one of the many available selling how-to books.)

Based on your "buyer's" motivations, you should be

able to form some idea of what a match might look like. There may be an existing initiative that seems a perfect fit with your prospect's priorities. Alternatively, you may decide that his resources and your institution's capabilities could provide the basis for a new venture addressing your mutual goals. It's good to have thought through in advance what opportunities might be of interest to a prospect. But beware the "Chinese menu" approach. Your focus shouldn't be on the list itself, but rather, on the potential impact of the gift.

Let me cite a personal example; call it a "cranky donor" story, featuring me. My great-grandmother financed a small hospital in 1908. Originally named after her, it was renamed when rebuilt in the '70s. Now the hospital was building a "guest home" for families that were visiting patients, and had decided to name it in honor of her. They invited her extended family to attend the grand opening—which on the face of it must have seemed like a good idea. After all: weren't we a group that was predisposed to be supportive?

The problem was that my wife Fredi and I received a dressed-up form letter offering us "a few opportunities" to give, ranging from a guest suite ($15,000) to a tranquility garden ($75,000). To put it bluntly, I was annoyed. Why? First, there was no indication that any thought had been given to us, personally, or to our interests. Second, the letter failed to explain why the guest home was an important resource. (This is an easy case to make. Hospital visits are traumatic for families; many can't afford accommodations, and so on.). While we wanted to give because of our family connection, that sort of mission-related message was needed to make a compelling case to the average donor.

As it turned out, we ended up picking and supporting an "opportunity" on the list, but we probably would have done more if someone had bothered to call us, learn about our interests, and perhaps even suggest something in particular that we might be interested in.

Before leaving the topic of mission, message and money, I should acknowledge that there will be times when a prospect's interests and the organization's purpose simply do not align; there is no match to be made. That's O.K. You're sometimes better off helping the individual find something personally meaningful than pushing your agenda or just shutting the door. I've gotten some good "tips" for my cause (yes, with dollar signs attached) from people who were grateful for my honesty and assistance.

HOW IMPORTANT IS IT?

Talk to most fundraisers, and you'll likely hear the size of a gift discussed in terms of *absolute dollars*, and/or *considered from the perspective of the organization*. It's an understandable way of thinking—after all, you *do* have that ambitious overall goal in sight—but I believe it's ultimately a counterproductive one.

I've already made a point of using the term "significant gift," rather than "major gift." Why? Because I strongly believe that you have to *think about the gift from the donor's perspective, and in relative terms.* The question is the degree of sacrifice involved given the person's financial means—his or her willingness to "stretch"—and *not* the number of zeroes on the check.

Thinking this way leads naturally to a very different way of categorizing, targeting and approaching prospects. You can divide individual giving into three "importance categories": core, priority, and checkbook projects.[7] Look at **Table 2-1.**

TABLE 2-1: INDIVIDUAL GIVING CATEGORIES

Project importance	Number of projects supported	Personal funds devoted as % of giving	
Core	1-3	30-60%	
Priority	3-7	20-30%	← **Significant gift target**
Checkbook	25-100	5-15%	

---

[7] Two HBS students (Katie Cunninham and Marc Ricks)conducting a field study project about charitable gifts ranging from $10,000 to $10 million saw the same patterns, and came up with the names for the three categories.

Starting from the bottom, *checkbook* donations reflect a sincere but passing interest. You (as a donor) are swept up in the excitement of a telethon. Your work colleague asks you to sponsor her in a Walk for Hunger event. Someone who has donated to your cause asks you to reciprocate with a check for his. A donor may make a large number of such contributions, but the level of engagement and support will be low. An individual is likely to make more significant and less numerous gifts to causes he feels are important, and represent a personal *priority*. (Educational institutions count on this kind of giving when they tap their alumni.) To qualify for a *core* gift—and warrant a major sacrifice—the cause must be a true passion. Funding for an institute dedicated to finding a cure for a loved one's disease would be one example.

To cut directly to the chase, I believe that *priority projects should be the focus of significant fundraising efforts.*

Maybe you're thinking: *why not go for the core gifts?* It's a reasonable question, and one that the HBS campaign staff posed when I proposed focusing on the priority category. My response was, first, that those kinds of gifts are few and far between, and are usually devoted to something deeply attached to the donor's identity. Second, large donors have many giving opportunities, and are barraged with countless legitimate proposals, probably including requests from organizations more specifically focused on their interests. Third, "once in a lifetime gifts" often are just that: a legacy gift later in life, sometimes from individuals without much of a giving history. For all these reasons and more, I argue that it's better to go after a relatively easy target—a priority gift.

I developed my version of the priority-giving strategy after a capital campaign experience with the late Frank Batten, an HBS Class of 1952 alum and media pioneer. As the publisher of a newspaper in Virginia in the 1950s, he had championed desegregation; the paper earned a Pulitzer Prize for that work. He also was a noted philanthropist, making large gifts to his undergraduate alma mater and many other institutions and causes.

As I waited outside his office, I considered what to say to Frank. If I went about the conversation the normal way, explaining how important HBS and the campaign were, I suspected we'd just get into an argument. (Frank wasn't one for tooting one's own horn, so I figured I shouldn't toot HBS's horn.) I decided to try a different tack, and begin by telling Frank how proud the School was of his success, and appreciative of his contributions to so many worthy causes. This was easy, because it was true. I closed by saying that I hoped HBS could be number four or five on his list of giving priorities. Not long afterward, HBS received a $32 million donation from Frank to support the renovation of the School's residential campus.

Actually, that put HBS *fifth* on Frank's list—but that turned out to be a very good place to be!

Over the years, I've heard lots of confirmation of the effectiveness of the priority-gift strategy. The experience of Groton, an independent boarding school in Massachusetts, provides one example. During Groton's capital campaign, which was approximately one-tenth the size of HBS's, the headmaster of that school enjoyed great success by asking people to make Groton the number-four priority on their giving lists. Conversely, I recently attended a meeting of a group to which I was a reasonably generous donor—in fact, one of their biggest—and was offended to hear a staff member proclaim that this organization had to be the *number-one priority of everyone at the table!* Why? And who was he to make that decision for me?

Would it be wonderful, even magical, to become a prospect's number-one priority? Absolutely! Would it be wonderful, even magical, if that prospect's engagement with your organization grew and grew, and your work emerged as his or her core issue? Yes—all the better!

Copyright Grantland Enterprises; www. grantland.net

Meanwhile, don't count on wonders and magic. Be bold, ambitious, and realistic. Earn the bird in your hand, and keep an eye on the two birds in the bush.

CHAPTER 3

ARE YOU WELL MANAGED?

For some potential donors, no question is more important than this one: *Are you well managed?*

And let's face it: they have reason to be concerned. A succession of stories emerging from mismanaged charities—for example, the princely compensation package awarded to the former head of United Way back in the early 1990s, and more recent headline-grabbing missteps by United Way chapters at the state level—all have contributed to an understandable wariness within the donor community.

I am constantly amazed by two things: 1) how little attention most charitable organizations pay to key management issues, and 2) how few of them are transparent about their finances. Many nonprofit brochures and reports read like the cartoon below. True, Charity Navigator and other watchdog groups have put themselves forward as independent evaluators of nonprofit organizations' performance. This is all to the good, but it's not enough. Donors need to get the story from *you*. Do you know what you're doing? Are you wasting your current resources, meaning that you'll be very likely to waste mine? Will you be around next month?

Copyright Grantland Enterprises; www.grantland.net

These may sound like harsh questions, but they're not. Smart investors in the philanthropic field know that charities don't usually fail because they lack talent, passion, or purpose; typically, they fail through mismanagement. Few people knowingly invest in a venture that is being managed toward failure.

What kind of case do you have to make, regarding the quality of your management? In part, the answer depends on your target audiences, and their level of managerial sophistication. Some prospects just need reassurance that your organization's economics are in order, and that your money is going toward its intended purposes. You can address this through transparency. For example: you can go well beyond the IRS-required form 990 in your annual reporting of your organization's financial affairs. A detailed annual report may feel like a burden on your already overtaxed staff, but it may be exactly what's needed to make your case. That proved to be true for us at Harvard Business School. We published our first-ever annual report during our capital campaign, in no small part to help alumni understand why their gifts were essential to the advancement of the School's mission.

More sophisticated audiences may demand more. They may want evidence of good management that goes beyond the numbers. For example: What about governance? Do you have an effective leadership team? How do you define success? How do you track it? Do you have a strategic plan? Is it linked in compelling ways to your various units' operational plans? Do you have the infrastructure required to support your current operations? How about your longer-term plans? Do you have the talent you need, and a way to develop the capabilities you will need, from within and beyond your organization? Do you have a robust succession plan?

These are the things that a more sophisticated—and a more *significant*—donor may be looking for, and therefore, they are things to which you as a nonprofit leader should be paying attention. Put simply, you have to be "businesslike" to appeal to people who have made their own money. In 2011, there was a *New York Times* headline that read, "Madonna's Charity Fails in Bid to Finance School."[8] The charity (Raising Malawi) had amassed $18 million to build an academy for girls in Malawi. Amid allegations of mismanagement, the executive director of the charity had already resigned. Now the board of directors was being ousted. The real tragedy: millions of valuable donor dollars were unaccounted for, and a worthy project was being abandoned.

Of course, the notion of using business-oriented approaches in the nonprofit sector is not a new one, and there are many good examples of this philosophy in action. In my experience, the best results begin with the assumption that every nonprofit exists to *deliver value*, as defined by its mission. How does that happen? There are at least three good answers, starting with a sound *economic model*. "No margin, no mission," is how a nun in charge of a hospital once phrased it. Ray Gilmartin—a good friend

---

[8] "Madonna's Charity Fails in Bid to Finance School," Adam Nagourney, *New York Times*, March 24, 2011.

with extensive experience in both the for-profit and philanthropic sectors—advises the people on whose boards he sits that they should think of themselves as "tax-exempt" rather than "non-profit," to underscore that good management principles are vitally important to their enterprises.

In addition, value-delivery depends to a great extent on effective management of the *human dimension* of the organization. (This is especially true in the philanthropic realm. As you probably know very well already, philanthropy is a very complicated sport, with many players and agendas!) Finally, I believe that delivering value requires an *entrepreneurial approach*, with the pursuit of opportunities being at the very core of your management style.

Let's look at each of these contributors to value-delivery in turn.

THE ECONOMIC DIMENSION

Of all the things that you could focus on at work today, what would you find most interesting and rewarding? Most likely, your answer has something to do with your *mission*: the impact your school turnaround project is having, your plans to open a new medical clinic in a rural area, the premiere of your next arts performance, or whatever the specifics.

But how about your financial plans? Maybe financial planning isn't at the top of your list. After all, it's a dry world—full of numbers and formulas, rather than people and purpose. And it's a world that you and your colleagues may understand only imperfectly, and in which you spend no more time than is absolutely necessary.

And yet, a big part of your leadership role is to develop an economic model that is appropriate to your mission and context, and make sure that it is transparent to all.

I've witnessed firsthand the perils of not tending to one's economic model. Here's a common mistake: big dreams coupled with inadequate resources. How does that happen? In some cases, an organization builds up a big infrastructure—people, systems, space—in anticipation of significant growth. If that growth fails to occur, the organization "hits the wall." Program proliferation (also known as "mission creep") also can cause problems if the economics are not properly considered, because an ever-larger menu of small things will eventually cost you scale economies. Finally, there's the old standby of financial brinksmanship, whereby an organization with a group of loyal and generous supporters routinely overspends, and then passes the hat with an air of desperation in its communications: *Help! We're going under!*

Eventually, you *do* go under.

For a whole host of reasons, nonprofits tend not to understand their economics. Many lack financial expertise, and don't appreciate the fundamentals. Many don't do formal strategic or financial planning, and lack discipline around cash flow, income statements, and balance sheets. Others tend to extrapolate from the past, rather than examining their environments and looking to the future. Some just plain don't pay attention.

I believe that changing those attitudes and practices— and building relevant capabilities—should be a priority for you in your leadership position. Why? Because understanding the underlying economics of the service model you've adopted, and being vigilant in assessing the impact of environmental changes on it, are essential to your continued success. (A friend who serves on several nonprofit boards likes to encourage them to think of their organizations as "tax exempt" rather than "nonprofit," to underscore the point that the principles of good business and management practices still apply.)

Your economic model needs to yield a "bottom line" that makes your mission financially viable. Managing expenses is important, of course. But our focus here is on the "top line"—that is, how to garner the financial resources you need to pursue the opportunities you have targeted. There are many ways to get there. *Fundraising*, for example, counts on philanthropy (event-driven, periodic, or planned) to fuel the machine. *Memberships* can be another source of support, providing support on an ongoing basis. *Earned income* can come in through a number of pipelines: fees for core services; ancillary services (like the Harvard Business School's publishing company or the Boston Ballet's school); transactions, such as sponsorships for Walk for Hunger; and repetitive income, like endowment earnings.

A nonprofit's economic model includes a mix of income sources, but is dominated by one type. Let's look at some examples, including SummerSearch (a philanthropic model), National Public Radio (an earned income model), and Sudbury Valley Trustees (a membership model).

A philanthropic model: SummerSearch. Approximately 86 percent of SummerSearch's costs are covered by fundraising, with the remaining 14 percent being met by in-kind scholarships for summer programs. Philanthropic giving is dominated by individuals (60 percent), then foundations (35 percent), and corporations (5 percent).

SummerSearch's example illustrates how a model can change over time. The organization's fundraising traditionally reflected the organization's decentralized model, with each city-based chapter appealing to donors concerned about local youth. In recent years, though, SummerSearch's increasing scale began to raise some new fundraising challenges and opportunities. The organization's national organization and initiatives were funded through modest assessments on local groups—a "fee for core services," if you will—but that was starting to prove inadequate. At that point, SummerSearch began trying to establish a national endowment, which meant fundraising "above" the local level. In time, given an even stronger track record, they hoped to be able to add government funding to their mix.

An earned income model: NPR. NPR represents 18 percent of the national public radio system, including local stations. Programming fees from local stations and satellite distribution fees traditionally have accounted for half of its income. With on-air and direct mail solicitation prohibited, it has relied on corporate sponsorships for another 40 percent of its income. All told, therefore, some 90 percent of NPR's income is earned, with endowment income and foundation grants accounting for the remaining 10 percent.

But a number of environmental factors that arose in recent years began to challenge that model. Corporate funding—always vulnerable to larger economic swings—began to drop off in the recent recession. In response, NPR launched its first-ever major gifts campaign. This raised an interesting question: who do big donors belong to—NPR, or the local stations? Technology, and specifically the ability to stream content from one station nationally, was changing relationships. For example: a station in Washington state became well known for its outstanding jazz programming, and—via the web—began attracting aficionados from many other stations' listening areas. To whom would those listeners donate? With technology advances, longstanding allegiances were in peril, but new opportunities presented themselves as well.

A membership model: Sudbury Valley Trustees (SVT). This Eastern Massachusetts organization was founded in 1953, when a Marine Corps veteran returning home noticed that the open spaces that had characterized his home town of Wayland were being lost to housing developments and malls. He sent a form letter to the residents of Wayland and neighboring Sudbury, inviting them to become members of the newly formed "Sudbury Valley Trustees" for $3.00. SVT was run entirely by volunteers, and through an advocacy campaign, it was able to convince most towns in the Sudbury River valley to adopt flood plain zoning measures. In 1981, SVT's founder became its first paid employee when he took the post of executive director. Over time, SVT expanded the scope of its mission—land conservation and the protection of wildlife habitats—to comprise 36 communities in the Concord, Assabet, and Sudbury River basins. A 17-person, community-based voluntary board was established.

From advocacy and education, SVT moved into land acquisition, which required close collaboration among landowners, businesses, other local conservation agencies, and government agencies. By 2008, through gift or purchase, it had acquired 72 properties comprising 2,200 acres, including reservations open to the public for walking, cross-country skiing, canoeing, bird watching, and horseback riding; and had assembled an additional 1,100 acres on which it held conservation restriction rights, protecting the land from further development. SVT also played a key role in earmarking an additional 6,000 acres for permanent protection by public agencies. Between 1953 and the present, SVT has raised approximately $12 million for operations and an additional $10 million for land projects. Looked at from another angle, the land protected by SVT has consumed about $1,200 per acre in charitable contributions—land that is probably worth $100,000 an acre today.

SVT's annual memberships—which increased over the years to more than 3,600—were sufficient to cover an annual budget (in 2011) of $951,000. For big acquisitions, SVT solicited funds directly from abutters to the targeted properties. It was an extremely efficient financial model, but as the group's landholdings grew, so did the cost and complexity of managing those properties. As a result, SVT undertook to raise an endowment to help meet the costs of land stewardship. It also decided that it couldn't—and shouldn't—try to "do it all." It began establishing a network of partners who could provide needed expertise (e.g., pro bono legal services, other local conservation groups, and the Environmental Protection Agency (and other government agencies) for projects and ongoing activities. It also rallied more than 150 volunteers, and organized projects to help with hands-on conservation work. This model allowed SVT to exert a much greater impact than it otherwise could have with a staff of only nine, a small annual budget, and approximately $3 million in total annual donations and land purchase gifts.

Within these broad categories, every nonprofit has its unique financial model. Some, as we've seen, evolve over time. Others combine elements of several of these models.

For an example of a relatively complex model, see the story below about Mount Auburn Hospital. This is an institution that has managed to survive and thrive over more than a century, in part due to its remarkable ability to adapt to dramatic and ongoing changes in the health care industry. Mount Auburn's story illustrates the importance not only of effective financial planning, but also of the "people factor."

MOUNT AUBURN HOSPITAL

Mount Auburn Hospital was founded in 1886 in Cambridge, Massachusetts as a charitable institution, and began to attract paying customers at the turn of the century. It had a longstanding relationship with Harvard Medical School; Mount Auburn physicians were on the Harvard faculty, and the hospital hosted teaching programs. That made it an unusual hybrid: a mix of suburban community hospital and large medical-center hospital.

As health care costs in the U.S. spiraled in the 1970s, the industry responded with managed care, whereby Health Maintenance Organizations (HMOs) or other organizations would enroll individuals in comprehensive medical plans, take a more active role in patient care, and spread the risk to providers. In the 1980s, managed care organizations and federal and state governments further clamped down on costs. Mount Auburn responded by becoming one of the first Boston-area hospitals to contract with a commercial payer to "manage care;" restructuring the way it provided services, tracked patients, and utilized equipment; and investing $20 million to build a referral network of primary care physicians (PCPs).

In the early 1990s, a number of Boston hospitals were forced to close their doors. Anticipating industry consolidation, health care providers began forming their own networks. Recognizing its vulnerability, Mount Auburn convened a task force that concluded the hospital should seek a partner *now*, while still in a strong financial and market position. In 1996, Mount Auburn joined the CareGroup organization. The board also initiated a $25 million renovation project that would strengthen the hospital in targeted areas.

In the near term, though, Mount Auburn was struggling. Modest operating surpluses turned into steep operating losses amounting to $10 million by 1998. Cost reduction measures heightened longstanding tensions between Mount Auburn's CEO and its medical staff; two major groups of doctors left. In 1998, the CEO resigned, and the board named an interim replacement.

MOUNT AUBURN HOSPITAL (CONT.)

Jeanette Clough was recruited from Waltham Hospital, where she was CEO, for the same spot at Mount Auburn. As a woman and a former nurse, she encountered some skepticism from traditionalists, but effectively reached out to employees and won their trust. Several of her senior managers chose to leave amid the leadership change, but the exodus allowed her to build a new team.

Clough gave herself three years to turn around the hospital's financials. She put in mechanisms to tackle bad debt and denied insurance claims, and maximize revenues under case-rate systems. She partnered with medical leadership to improve business metrics in each department. In her second year, Mount Auburn broke even; in 2004 and 2005, it ranked among the state's top five hospitals in operating margins.

With the near-term crisis resolved, leadership turned its attention to the future. Mount Auburn was one of the last two hospitals in the state to still have four-bed rooms, and its interventional cardiac catherization lab was outdated. Plans were made for an $80 million expansion of the main building, and introduction of cutting-edge technology. In 2004, a $21 million, five-year capital campaign was launched. By the end of 2007, $24 million had been raised. In November 2008, Mount Auburn opened its new 150,000-square-foot building.

Mount Auburn now has 205 licensed beds; provides comprehensive inpatient services in all medical specialties; is developing centers of excellence in women's services, heart care, and cancer care; and offers a variety of inpatient and outpatient clinical services. Leadership remains committed to the hospital's dual mission of providing excellent care with compassion for the residents of Cambridge and surrounding communities through "high tech, high touch" services, and contributing to the development of top-notch physicians and health professionals through residency and health care teaching programs.

THE HUMAN DIMENSION

I've spoken much about planning but planning is done by and for organizations, and organizations are made up of people. As Oklahoma Senator James Inhofe has pointed out, "People are, well, only human." People make organizations vital, useful, and *complicated*.

At its simplest, philanthropy involves donors, volunteers, and staff, both within and beyond your organizational boundaries. Volunteers provide leadership for direction-setting and fundraising (e.g., board members), or serve as "extra pairs of hands," providing pro bono services or critical fundraising support. Nonprofit staff performs many functions: participation in direction setting and fundraising leadership, operational planning and management, delivery of services, fundraising support, and coordination of volunteers. Donors bring not only resources but—hopefully—a passion for the organization's mission, and a willingness to champion it.

Roles can overlap, which may offer flexibility and synergies. Volunteers often are donors—which raises a thorny question. Should board members be required to make a financial contribution at specified level? Opinions on this vary, but I believe that board members should be expected to give according to their means. (It's important to lead by example.) But not all contributions are financial in nature. Your best fundraiser may be someone who's not able to make a large donation personally—now, or ever. A board member may be able to offer much-needed expertise, and thereby help the organization avoid paying market price for that expertise. Obviously, this is just as valuable as a cash contribution.

Sometimes, overlapping roles can cause confusion or conflict. A big donor feels she should have decision-making power; who's really in charge? The executive director is running the organization like a private fiefdom; who's watching the mission, and rallying the troops? In general, organizational members need to be clear about their distinctive roles, and about which hat they're wearing in any given situation.

As a board member, I once gave an individual within the company—call him John—a customized pentagonal dodecahedron (that is, an object with 12 faces, all of which are pentagons, something like a squared-off soccer ball). On each face of the object, I wrote one of John's many roles: shareholder, CEO, son of the founder, and so on. There were plenty—in fact, one for each edge. Every time John came by to talk, I made him point to which hat he was wearing. In the for-profit and nonprofit sectors alike, clarity is important!

In a strong nonprofit, everyone works in partnership, bound together by a shared commitment to the mission of the organization. At the same time, people also have their own needs and agendas—their own "gives" and "gets." At the highest level, the "give" is attending to an unfilled social need, and the "get" is a feeling of commitment and satisfaction. Volunteers donate their time and talents; in exchange, they get an outlet for their talents, recognition for their work, and a meaningful way to spend their time. Donors get a receipt, and—presumably—whatever result they are hoping for from their contribution. Staff members get a paycheck, and—again, hopefully—more.

I say "hopefully" because nonprofits often are not able to pay market wages, and have to count on their participants to be motivated by nonfinancial factors. The New Teacher Project—a national nonprofit dedicated to closing the achievement gap by ensuring that high-need students get outstanding teachers—specifically recognized the value of "soft" incentives in a job description for a site manager in Nashville, Tennessee:

We also offer a motivated team of colleagues, a collegial atmosphere that values professional development... [and] the opportunity to impact the direction of a growing, mission-driven company that is committed to the success of our nation's children.[9]

---

[9] Source: The New Teacher Project's employment website, http://tbe.taleo.net/NA5/ats/careers/requisition.jsp?org=THENEWTEACHERPROJECT&cws=1&rid last accessed April 16, 2011.

It is a mistake, though, to ignore the fact that a nonprofit job is still a job, and that most people need to earn a living. When the teachers at a small Vermont school in an expensive resort area approached their board to request a long overdue cost-of-living salary increase, the response they got was, in so many words, "If you can't afford to work here for free, you shouldn't be working here." Board members clearly saw it as a "gentleman's" profession.

Copyright Grantland Enterprises; www. grantland.net

NPR, in contrast, tries to attract top talent by offering market-rate compensation and benefits, based on salary surveys for comparable positions in the for-profit and nonprofit industries. My point in reciting these examples is that it is important to be clear on what motivates nonprofit participants, and especially your front-line troops. By maximizing individual motivation and keeping everyone focused on the mission, you'll get the best out of every employee, and keep your best ones.

Before leaving the topic of people, I have to report that I have seen far too many nonprofits that have degenerated into boiling cauldrons of politics and pettiness. An example: a development officer I was working with had an outstanding reputation for developing strategies for prospects. Unfortunately, he never seemed to get around to *implementing* them. "Ready, aim... ready, aim... ready, aim," was how one colleague described the problem. Eventually, I asked him if I could reassign a donor to someone who would actually pull the trigger. The reaction: howls of protest, to the effect of, "Hey—that's *my* prospect, he's on *my* list!" If you find this sort of unproductive competitiveness within your organization, ask yourself whether that attitude is being reinforced by your performance metrics, evaluation and compensation systems, or culture. If so, you can probably find ways to correct the problem.

Organizational structure also can contribute to unhealthy competition. I'm regularly amazed at how "siloed" nonprofits tend to be, especially in their fundraising groups. Within individual giving, there may be major-gift, annual-gift, planned-giving, and capital-campaign groups. Each group may be fighting for "donor rights." At best, they lose an opportunity to pool thinking and resources for the benefit of the institution and donors themselves. At worst, they harass and confuse a prospective donor through multiple, contradictory contacts.

But take heart; siloes can be torn down. At HBS, for

example, I restructured the traditional groups into cross-functional, donor-centered teams, with good results.

AN ENTREPRENEURIAL APPROACH

What does "being entrepreneurial" mean? And what does it look like in a nonprofit setting? Let me offer a few tools and examples. First, at the organizational level, is an *entrepreneurial model* that will help you scan your own organization and your environment. Next, at the individual level, is an *entrepreneurial mindset* that will help you think about how to behave as a leader and manage your nonprofit business.

I must begin though with an important caveat. The trend toward applying business practices—including entrepreneurship—in the nonprofit setting has had mixed results. For all the similarities between for-profit and nonprofit ventures, there are some important differences. The goal of business is said to be to maximize shareholder value (although most successful business people I know would say they "serve the customer at a profit"); nonprofits strive to deliver social value. Markets strive for efficiency; in the nonprofit sector, that can seem to be in conflict with fairness and equity. Business decisions are (supposedly) rational; nonprofit decisions often have emotional drivers, as well. Decision impacts differ—for example, discontinuing a critical social service is much more serious than pulling a brand of shampoo off the shelves. So nonprofits have to move carefully and wisely when they seek to adapt successful business models to their unique needs.

But—I argue—*they still have to move... and in an entrepreneurial way.*

An Entrepreneurial Model

Entrepreneurship, in a for-profit or nonprofit setting, can be thought of as consisting of four building blocks: people, context, deal, and opportunity. I refer to them collectively as the "PCDO" model of entrepreneurship. (See **Figure 3—1**) Understanding these elements, and the need for alignment among them, is important for ventures of all shapes and sizes. And understanding that they form a dynamic system—with a change in one element having repercussions across the others and perhaps determining the fate of the whole venture—is even more important. While conveniently divided into four components, they are continually interacting and changing over time.

Let's look at these four building blocks separately, and in combination. Then we'll consider how they relate to our four donor questions.

FIGURE 3-1: THE PCDO MODEL OF SOCIAL ENTREPRENEURSHIP

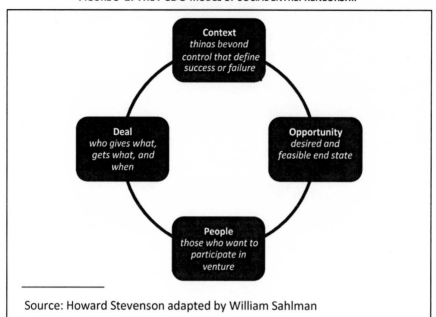

Source: Howard Stevenson adapted by William Sahlman

The external **context** is the starting point for an entrepreneurial venture. It is "out there," in the real world, where you first detect a need for change, and—if all goes well—find a way to make that change on a sustainable economic basis. Broadly speaking, your context includes such things as macroeconomics, geopolitical and sociocultural environments, science and technology, and tax and regulatory affairs. They are largely beyond your control, but they can spell success or failure for your efforts. So the most successful entrepreneurs tend to be those who are always watching their environment, and considering the implications of what they see there. They ask themselves questions like: *What is going on in the world that we can and should* *respond to? What are we uniquely equipped to do about it? Who should we be comparing ourselves to?*

Defining the **opportunity** is at the heart of what an entrepreneur does. An opportunity represents a desirable *and* feasible future state, and requires changing the status quo. It is created by addressing a contextual need with available (or obtainable) resources. The right scale of effort is critical for both credibility and impact. "Ending world hunger" is almost certainly too grand. On the other hand, "improving health, education, and economic capacity in these five Bangladeshi villages" may be a realistic shorter term opportunity, and—if you can pull it off—the foundation of a much bigger program. Brazilian social entrepreneur Denis Mizne began with a dream of ending gun violence near a local school. Twelve years later, it had grown into a national gun disarmament movement that had helped reduce gun violence by 80 percent in Sao Paulo.

At an early stage in the definition and pursuit of an opportunity, you will need to sketch out a sensible plan for addressing it, and then go seek allies who can help you define the idea more fully. Engaging these constituencies in the effort to define the opportunity is likely to increase their enthusiasm and commitment, which may be vitally important to your work. In nonprofits, even more than for-profits, a common purpose—the desire to have an impact on a particular social issue—is a linchpin.

What are the implications for fundraising? Context and opportunity are important considerations in answering two of our four donor questions: *Are you doing important work? Will my gift make a difference?* Donors must first be convinced that there is a real need in the world to be addressed (from their perspective), and then that your joint pursuit of an opportunity to address it will have a meaningful impact.

Choosing the right **people** to get involved is the next key building block. And here I'm not just talking about sources of funds (although that certainly is important!). You will need not only money from others, but also talent, time, and networks. The right people may include a top-notch executive director for your organization; a leading expert from a government agency for an environmental project; volunteers to sort food, or to tutor at an elementary school; a pro bono consultant to help you develop your strategy; a board member to step up to lead your capital campaign; or another nonprofit with complementary services to meet the additional needs of your clients. The first question to ask yourself is: *What do we need?* Then, *Who can provide that?* And finally, *Why should they?*

Choosing the right people is a prerequisite to being

able to answer another key donor question: *Are you well managed?* Your organization must have the capacity—including leadership—to survive, thrive, and fulfill your promises to donors and social beneficiaries alike.

That last question introduces the notion of the **"deal"**—a word that for some people has negative connotations. It shouldn't. The "deal" simply defines who in a venture gives what, who gets what, and when that will happen. All enterprises, nonprofits and for-profits alike, engage in transactions that are voluntary exchanges of tangibles (e.g., money or goods) or intangibles (e.g., respect or peace of mind). Accomplishing almost anything of importance involves a complex set of "give/gets" among participants over time. This, in turn, requires a clear understanding what each person has to offer, what motivates them, and why they want to play in this particular game.

And that, in turn, is important to being able to answer the donor question, *Will this be a satisfying experience for me?* The notion of the deal is particularly important for the art of fundraising.

As a fundraising leader, you too are a participant, so you have to understand clearly why *you* are involved. You can join a symphony board for the social networking, love of the music, respect for the institution, or love of your cello-playing grandson. All are valid reasons that can be fulfilled (the "get"), but they may lead you to quite different levels and types of involvement (the "give").

A key part of a nonprofit organization's success stems from its effectiveness at adjusting and readjusting these elements as the organization grows and evolves, and as its context changes. That is what I mean by the *dynamic* nature of entrepreneurship. A change in one element impacts another, which impacts another, and so on. Keep in mind, too, that the interactions are not just one-way. A change in your environment can change your "menu" of opportunities. At the same time, your success at pursuing a given opportunity can change the environment in which you operate.

Look at **Figure 3-2**, which looks something like a map of a cyclone. And in fact, if your nonprofit is like most, most of the elements of your world are in motion, most of the time.

FIGURE 3-2: THE PCDO MODEL OF SOCIAL ENTREPRENEURSHIP "IN MOTION"

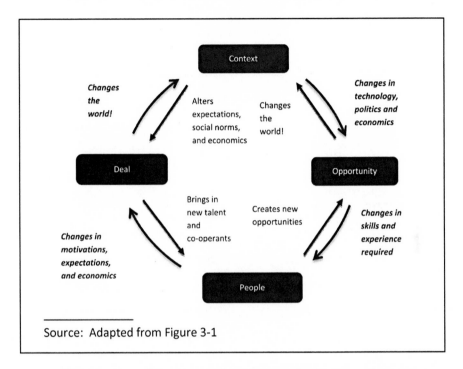

Source: Adapted from Figure 3-1

Starting at the top and moving clockwise, changes in context can yield new opportunities, which tend to require a distinct set of skills, experience, and contacts to exploit them. The people tapped to fill those needs bring with them motivations, expectations, and resources that will have to be negotiated into a collaboration to change the world. Starting again at the top and moving counterclockwise, changes in the environment may change expectations and social norms, providing the impetus for new collaborations (deals and people) to pursue opportunities to change the world.

In reality, of course, things don't necessarily progress all the way "around the clock face," and they rarely stop after only one cycle. A single organization is likely to go through multiple cycles as it grows. And even within a stable context, there is likely to be a certain amount of turbulence. For example, there may be people changes that prompt changes in the structure of the deal.

SummerSearch, which was mentioned earlier, offers an interesting example of a nonprofit that has grown through a "snowball" approach that is typical of entrepreneurial ventures. Along the way, it has attempted to continually align and realign the elements of its entrepreneurial model, while keeping its eye on the prize: helping disadvantaged urban youth change their lives. As you read the short case history below, ask yourself how SummerSearch has (or hasn't) addressed the opportunities and challenges implied in the model above. For example:

- Can it really change some piece of the world?
- Is it taking advantage of changing technology and socio-economics?
- Are new opportunities being created?
- Does it have the requisite skills and experience?
- Can it attract new players and talent?

In sum, the question is: will SummerSearch be able to survive and thrive as the organization grows and evolves, and its context changes?

SUMMERSEARCH

The story begins with Linda Mornell, an adolescent therapist working and living in the San Francisco area, in the 1980s. Her involvement with the school system had made her acutely aware of the challenges faced by urban youth, more than 90 percent minority students, trapped in a cycle of poverty. She was eager to be part of a solution to the problem. Linda also was a mother looking for enriching opportunities for her own children. She sent them to an experiential education program one summer, and was delighted with the impact it had on them.

Linda felt that low-income children also could benefit from, and deserved access to, the same summer program opportunity. In 1990, she arranged for scholarships for 14 inner city students; SummerSearch was born. When it became apparent that students needed more, and year-round, support, it expanded its mission. SummerSearch ultimately positioned itself as a leadership development program, with a unique commitment:

> The SummerSearch mission is to find resilient low-income high school students and inspire them to become responsible and altruistic leaders by providing year-round mentoring, life-changing summer experiences, college advising, and a lasting support network.

SummerSearch began with a core group of people committed to the cause and to Linda, and tried to attract more supporters. They cited facts on the individual and societal costs of poverty, and the importance of education as an antidote. Teachers, initially reticent, began identifying and recommending high-potential students, who were expected to give 150 percent to the program. This pre-qualification was attractive to SummerSearch partners, who wanted to support diversity and involve more minorities, but also wanted a good fit. Student participation grew, and talented staff and volunteers signed up.

SummerSearch knew that demonstration of the program's impact would be essential, but challenging. As a startup, its best metric was

SUMMERSEARCH (CONT.)

completion of the program. Over time, it developed a track record, and conducted assessment and longitudinal studies. Many partners and volunteers were directly involved with students, and could witness firsthand their enthusiasm, and accomplishments. SummerSearch also organized events allowing students to directly interact with donors, who were impressed and moved by the experience. Donor ranks, initially family and friends, expanded. Foundations and corporations became interested.

As San Francisco flourished, grassroots efforts sprang up in other cities. The Boston program, the first replication of the SummerSearch model, was founded by my wife, Fredi Stevenson, in 1996. She was looking for an impactful volunteer opportunity. Boston's soon-to-be-named executive director had just graduated from Divinity School, but didn't want to be a preacher; and needed to be in Boston because his wife was in medical school there. They both were interested in serving children, and impressed with SummerSearch, so it seemed a good fit. It was. By 2009, the Boston program had grown from serving 13 students to serving more than 375 students, and was on track to reaching its goal of reaching students in every qualified Boston Public High School.

SummerSearch spread to six other cities. Each program operated independently, with strong local leadership, and each did its own fundraising. SummerSearch also had established a national group to provide shared services, such as administrative systems, and formed a national leadership group that included city executive directors. In 2009, total staff numbered approximately 95, and its total budget was approximately $12.5 million.

In 2010, SummerSearch celebrated its 20th anniversary as "a high-impact program that gives low-income students the opportunities and support they need to transform their lives, achieve their own potential, and create change as role models and everyday leaders." With almost 2,000 alumni, it now was serving approximately 1,050 students each year.

An Entrepreneurial Mindset

As noted above, I believe that for businesses and nonprofits alike, delivering value requires an *entrepreneurial mindset*, with the pursuit of opportunities being at the very core of your management style. What, exactly, does that mean?

Entrepreneurial management *is* different from other management approaches. Nevertheless, it can be located on a spectrum of management behaviors. (See **Figure 3-3**) This spectrum ranges from *Promoters* to *Trustees*—both words that I use in a particular way. *Promoters* are individuals who are supremely confident of their ability to seize an opportunity, whether or not the necessary resources are at hand. (Picture the prototypical inventor in his garage, or the director of a new women's support center.) *Trustees*, in contrast, are primarily concerned with preserving and utilizing existing resources. (Picture a manager in a large and well established business or foundation.) Entrepreneurial management tends toward the Promoter end of the spectrum, but still overlaps with administrative behaviors.

FIGURE 3-3: THE MANAGEMENT SPECTRUM

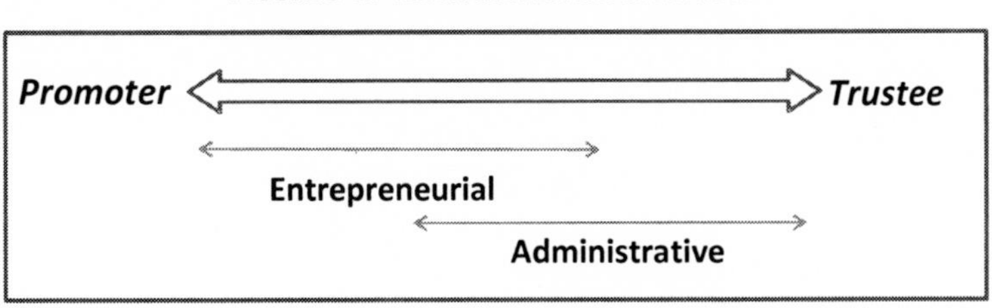

These two managerial approaches—entrepreneurial and administrative—vary along several key dimensions, including your strategic orientation; how you approach opportunities, how you control resources and manage relationships, and how you reward performance.[10] Let's look at each of these four points of differentiation in turn.

Strategic Orientation

Entrepreneurial managers take an outside-oriented approach to strategy development: *I will scan the horizon, and search for opportunity. After that, my fundamental task is to acquire the resources to pursue that opportunity.* They don't really have a choice, as they see it; if you eat what you kill, then you need to be constantly on the hunt for new prey. Administrative managers, by contrast, take a more inside-oriented approach, focusing on ways to use the resources at hand, and often not looking far beyond the organization's current scope of activities. It is so easy to lose sight of your mission, or fail to maintain your relevance in a changing world. At its worst, an inwardly focused nonprofit can become obsessed with perpetuating its existence.

---

[10] The management model described in this chapter is based on a HBS study described in *The Entrepreneurial Venture,* Harvard Business School Press, 1994 William A. Sahlman, Howard H. Stevenson, Michael J. Roberts, and Amar Bhide and the technical note *A Perspective on Entrepreneurship,* Howard Stevenson, HBS Note 384131 (rev 4/13/06).

Pursuing Opportunities

O.K.; you've found an opportunity—now what? Entrepreneurial managers are nimble, and willing to act quickly. They typically make their decisions based on a deep understanding of the field they're operating in, and they also consult within their network of colleagues and experts, as needed. They're comfortable making decisions on the fly, with less than perfect information. They're quick to get into a project, but equally quick to get out. They establish milestones and set goals, using them to measure how things are going.

An entrepreneur's approach to committing resources is *experimental*, in the sense that it is done in stages, with minimal exposure at each stage. Since nonprofits rarely have all the resources needed, the key is to use what you have to prove the value of your work and show progress to the people providing resources. An experimental approach also maximizes flexibility, and optimizes the use of scarce resources by allowing for just the right level of resources for the task at hand. It prevents an entrepreneur from overcommitting to things that just may not work or be too expensive to achieve Yes, a certain fearlessness is required; entrepreneurs take *managed risks*. Some failure is expected, but they learn from the experience: What went wrong? How can I avoid that in the future?

An administrative approach is more contemplative—and slower—about committing to an opportunity. It requires due diligence and reviews by committees and multiple levels of management. Once a bet is made, there will be a one-time, large-scale commitment of resources. It also may call for significant investment of political capital by the project's champion. Both kinds of investment make it difficult to pull the plug, even if the project isn't working—not demonstrating the desired results, or showing that it has a sustainable economic model—in its early stages.

Resources and Relationships

Because they face a chronic shortage of resources, entrepreneurs are always looking for creative solutions. For example, they get good at using other people's resources—not just in the tenuous early days of the venture, but also as they gain traction. They learn which resources they should own and employ, and which can be bartered, partnered, or rented. They pursue strategic alliances with other organizations. They recruit volunteers. They share mailing lists. They partner on projects. To accomplish that, entrepreneurial organizations tend to be "flat" and team-based, with information networks that support "co-opetition" throughout the internal and external system.

Administrative approaches focus mainly on existing resources. They tend to favor closed systems, where they have direct control over those resources. Administrative organizations often involve a formalized hierarchy. Jobs are tightly defined, with strict authorities and accountabilities. Information may be doled out on a "need to know" basis. Relationships with external parties are highly formalized.

Rewards

Rewards in entrepreneurial organizations are geared to achieving results, with individual, team, and organizational performance all linked. (Profit-sharing programs are one means to that end, but are not generally available to nonprofits.) Entrepreneurial organizations use rewards to encourage experimentation. Rewards at administrative organizations, by contrast, tend to be focused mainly on individual performance, and linked to job grades and descriptions. That can breed competitiveness, and discourage collaboration across organization levels and boundaries. Working together and sharing credit is particularly important for nonprofits.

Many ventures start out on the left end of the management spectrum, only to be pulled to the right. It may happen by design, or it may "just happen." For a start-up, this is a natural phenomenon. As you grow, you will need to put some sort of structure in place, aimed at 1) creating procedures to ensure consistency and quality, and 2) spreading best practices. For example, you will need to install accounting systems, think about a succession plan, and spend time on board reviews. But despite these necessary "shifts to the right"—toward the administrative model—you can still be entrepreneurial, as long as you're purposeful in those changes. Avoid the "it just happened" trap! Avoid the turf wars and layers of bureaucracy that lead to risk aversion and discourage your people from taking chances. *Don't let the cost of change become prohibitive.*

THREE ENTREPRENEURIAL EXAMPLES

Let's take a look at three nonprofits that embody the entrepreneurial model and mindset: the Clinton Foundation, the Gates Foundation, and the Metropolitan Opera. They all pay attention to PCDO components and dynamics, while using different managerial approaches to pursuing their missions. You can argue exactly where each might fall on the management spectrum, but their relative positioning is clear.

William J. Clinton Foundation

When *Fortune* did a feature story on the power of philanthropy, it commented that "Bill Gates has the money. But no one motivates people and moves mountains like Bill Clinton."[11] The Clinton Foundation began in a small office in Harlem, in 2001, with a vision of lowering the prices of HIV/AIDS medicines. Before long, its call to action had broadened, and its approach clarified:

Intelligence, ability, and aspiration are evenly distributed across societies—organization, investment, and opportunity are not. The William J. Clinton Foundation seeks to bridge this gap by using a business-oriented approach to address some of the world's greatest challenges.[12]

The initial Clinton HIV/AIDs Initiative was expanded, over the years, through initiatives focused on economic empowerment, education, the environment and energy, health systems and nutrition. , By 2009, it had grown into a worldwide organization with 559 paid staff plus volunteers working in more than 170 countries, and in all 50 United States, with an annual budget of $246 million.

Clinton's enterprise was based not on his own money, but on a powerful and diverse network of supporters

---

[11] *The Power of Philanthropy*, Bethany McLean, *Fortune* (9/18/2006), page 82.
[12] Clinton Foundation 2008 Annual Report, page 2.

drawn by his passion and prestige. *Collaboration* was a watchword. The Clinton Foundation prided itself on its entrepreneurial people and processes, and on its ability to leverage limited resources by working with likeminded partners. Its staff consisted of talented and highly motivated individuals, often from business. It didn't have a clear hierarchy or a detailed plan; it was driven more by needs and opportunities. It had a rough process for targeting and pursuing projects: the agenda was driven by Clinton himself; he and the foundation had to believe they could have an impact. If someone else was doing it better, Clinton's group either would back off, or consider partnering with them. If all signs were go, the Clinton Foundation would throw everything it could at the issue immediately—for example, enlist the key players, line up donors, and schedule the press conference. Then it would report on outcomes, metrics, and how it had done.

For all these reasons, I'd locate the Clinton Foundation far out on the left end—the entrepreneurial end—of our management spectrum.

Bill & Melinda Gates Foundation

What about Bill Gates, depicted in the *Fortune* article as Clinton's opposite? Was it even *possible* for the Gates Foundation—with its vast resources—to be entrepreneurial?

The Bill & Melinda Gates Foundation was created in 1994 with an initial stock gift of $94 million. Directed mainly by members of the Gates family, and inspired by their belief in the potential of science and technology to improve lives around the world, the foundation focused on initiatives in education and global health. Its founders instructed it to "take risks, make big bets, and move with urgency." By 2006, it was the largest grant-making foundation in the U.S., with assets approaching $30 billion; it also was able to leverage those assets by creating partnerships worldwide to accomplish specific initiatives. The foundation's staff of 300, housed on its Seattle campus, consisted of individuals hired for their expertise and experience, reputation for innovative solutions, belief in the mission, and comfort with change.

A critical turning point for the Gates Foundation came in June 2006, when Warren Buffet announced his $31 billion gift to the foundation, to be contributed in annual increments beginning two years hence. That gift essentially doubled the foundation's assets, and meant it would have to distribute something like $3 billion each year. This in turn meant that the organization would need to double its staff, build a new facility, and devise ways of distributing funds faster and in larger amounts—even while continuing its existing programs and starting up a new division focused on global development.

I think that the Gates Foundation has proven itself to be entrepreneurial, despite its enormous scale. To be sure, it is somewhere to the right of Clinton's on the management spectrum, but it is nonetheless an entrepreneurial venture.

But what would happen when Bill and Melinda were gone? They planned to contribute all their money before they died, and had specified that the Foundation's Trust must close within 50 years of their deaths. The terms of the Buffet gift required that at least one of the Gates be actively involved; a testimonial to the donor's confidence in his friends' vision and capabilities. A wander to the far right of the spectrum was not impossible, but did not seem likely.

The Met

The Metropolitan Opera Association of New York ("the Met") was founded in 1883 by a group of nouveaux riches—Roosevelts, Astors, Vanderbilts, and the like—as an alternative to the high society Academy of Music. It outlasted the latter to become the "most widely heard and known opera company in the world."[13] It prided itself on its track record of technological innovations, its commitment to artistic excellence, and a broad array of offerings. The Metropolitan Opera House at Lincoln

---

[13] www.metoperafamily.org/metopera/about (accessed 8/31/2009).

Center opened in 1966 with the latest of technical facilities. In 1995, the Met installed its own system of simultaneous translation for audience members, and developed a customer management system subsequently licensed and used by a large network of artistic organizations. Many of the Met's technology innovations were aimed at expanding the reach and appeal of opera: radio network broadcasting (1933), experimentation with television (1948), a regular series of performances on PBS (1997), and a 24-hour opera channel (2006).

"The Met's experiment of merging film with live performance has created a new art form... This venture may be the most significant in opera since the supertitle."[14] That was a *Los Angeles Times* reporter's take on *Metropolitan Opera: Live in HD* which featured transmissions of live high-definition productions to hundreds of movie theatres in more than a dozen countries. It was a bold venture that required new production skills, union agreements, movie theatre and media partnerships, and funding from a generous benefactor. It was heralded by the Met as part of a 2006-2007 transformation that "yielded strong results at the box office, reached new audiences, and garnered media acclaim and patron support."[15] Although media-earned

---

[14] The Los Angeles Times, 2/4/2007 as cited in The Met's 2006-07 Annual Report, page16.
[15] *Ibid.*

revenues still accounted for just 4 percent of operating revenue, they had increased nearly sevenfold: from $795,000 to $5.4 million. The Met's theatre partners—in many cases, historic movie houses that were eager for new offerings—benefited both from great publicity and a new revenue stream. Current opera buffs had a new way to indulge their passion, and new fans were being made. Despite its size and distinguished reputation, the Met proved itself ready, willing, and able to seize new opportunities.

The Met has remained true to its original mission while being innovative with technology. It seeks to broaden its market beyond opera house performances, which nevertheless remain its life blood. In my estimation, that earns them a spot to the right of the Clinton and Gates Foundations, but still with lively entrepreneurial tendencies.

So what can we learn from these examples of nonprofit management? One lesson is that entrepreneurial management—which is part of my larger prescription for how you should run your organization—can take many, many forms. Should you be more entrepreneurial or more administrative? The answer depends, in large part, on your organization and situation. But I would point out that the more entrepreneurial you are, the higher your impact per dollar spent.

Another, related lesson: no matter how much money you have, *every penny is precious*. The Gates Foundation's focused approach and attention to metrics underscores that fact. Bill and Melinda Gates don't have to worry much about keeping their donors happy—with the notable exception of Warren Buffet!—and still they insist upon stretching a buck, and demonstrating impact. You should, too.

And finally, perhaps the most striking lesson is the importance of adapting to change. *Anticipating* change, and responding proactively yields even better results.

I've always liked legendary business consultant W. Edwards Deming's observation about change. He approached the subject with his tongue firmly in his cheek. "It is not necessary to change," Deming commented. "Survival is not mandatory."

But if your cause is noble, good, unique, and impactful, survival *is* mandatory. Manage to make that happen!

CHAPTER 4

WILL MY GIFT MAKE A DIFFERENCE?

Let's say you've been having a great discussion—or even better, a series of productive discussions—with your prospect. She believes in the work you're doing, and respects your organization. In most cases, the last and major challenge in getting her to join your cause is to convince her that *her gift will make a difference.*

There are two levels to this discussion. First, you need to be able to build a rational case for why your organization needs the money and how you will use it. Next, you have to make it personal; it is *her* money, after all. You have to appeal to the prospective donor's head *and* heart.

WHY YOU NEED THE MONEY

To answer Question 1 to your donor's satisfaction, you had to present a clear and compelling mission. Now, you must convince her that the money you're asking for is essential for accomplishing your core mission. (In other words, it won't just go to support a peripheral project.) What's needed now—and what many organizations lack—is a mission-driven fundraising strategy. This requires systematic thinking. Have you translated your mission into a strategic plan, and rigorously assessed the resources required for its implementation? Have you thought broadly and creatively about financial sources, and identified any remaining gaps? What are your goals for fundraising? How will the funds be used?

This exercise will require close collaboration between your organization's development officers and its leadership, with lots of back-and-forth. What items on our financial-needs list do we think we have a reasonable chance of covering through fundraising? Activities not directly related to program outcomes are notoriously unattractive to donors. (Remember that people tend to draw this circle tightly. They may want to support "quality education," but they may *not* want to pay for an educational administrator.) How much do we expect to be able to raise for each of the targeted initiatives? And, finally: from which specific sources—grants, individual giving, and so on—do we expect to be able to get it?

After you've developed good answers to all these questions, you'll have to pull them together and present them in a way that resonates with donors. Most likely, you'll need an "umbrella" story that lays out your mission in a compelling way, with specific giving opportunities nested within that story, and sound reasons for the impact of the potential gifts.

Here's a question that you'll need to be prepared to deal with: *How will I know that my gift has made a difference?* The answer, in most cases, is complicated. Ideally, your plan will include specific performance metrics that can be tracked and reported back to donors. But measuring performance is a difficult and much-debated subject in the nonprofit world. Generally, inputs are easy to measure: "We raised $1 million; our revenues grew 43 percent." Outputs also are fairly easy to measure: "We ran 12 programs; we served 4,000 clients." Cause-and-effect relationships are far more elusive, especially in the kinds of work that most charitable organizations engage in. (If it's any consolation, scientists—who tend to control most of the variables in their work—also have a devilish time with cause and effect.) In fact, the hardest thing to measure is impact—and yet that's what significant donors are most interested in. So you need to look for good measures. Even in the absence of statistical "proof," though, there are tools at your disposal. Stories about and by beneficiaries, documentaries about the issue, personal visits—all are powerful ways to bring home the need and the impact.

Let's dig deeper by looking at how one organization tackles the measurement challenge. SummerSearch, introduced in earlier chapters, strives to help disadvantaged urban youth change their lives.

How, exactly, to measure outcomes against a goal that broad and ambitious? In its early years, the organization could only point to the number of students completing the summer experience: the higher, the better. As time passed, SummerSearch's leaders sought to add other metrics, including: (1) success at breaking the cycle of poverty (as evidenced by the percentage of students staying in the program through high school, graduating from high school, going to college, and completing college); and (2) success at creating positive leaders and role models (as evidenced by percentages of alumni who stay actively involved in SummerSearch, are involved in community service, and aspire/go on to careers in public service).

To my eye, the results are impressive. Here's the scorecard for 2009, averaged across SummerSearch's several affiliates:

- 99.6 percent of participants graduated high school, 96 percent of graduates went on to college, 89 percent of college students graduated or stayed on track to do so, and 92 percent were first-generation college students

- 72 percent of alumni were involved in service to the community, 221 attended SummerSearch's National Alumni Summit, 4 currently were on staff, and 14 percent made donations

The effort to develop additional metrics of impact continues. For example, SummerSearch also has initiated a five-year longitudinal study to help determine the extent to which it fosters long-term positive outcomes for young people, including educational attainment, economic self-sufficiency, and community engagement. And, of course, all of these measures are regularly complemented by strong anecdotal evidence—i.e., stories of individual success—and local activities that raise awareness in general and also enable donors to interact with students themselves.

DONORS' MONEY AT WORK

Only rarely does a significant gift come with no strings attached. Usually a use is specified, often in terms of support for a project or program. It is the fundraiser's job to take the general and turn it into the concrete: "*Your money at work.*" For some donors, the biggest concern is whether their gift will have adequate visibility. If you're raising money for a large institution, you may hear comments to the effect of, "For you guys, my money will be just a drop in the bucket. I'm sure I can have more impact, and do more good, at a smaller organization." If your institution is perceived as wealthy, you may hear, "Why should I give to *you*? You don't need it." In Harvard's case, I've never found it effective to say: "We're down to our last $26 billion." I usually start with: "I'm not asking you to give *to* Harvard, but *through* Harvard. Together, we can do things we cannot do alone."

We certainly encountered this sort of skepticism during the HBS capital campaign. Early research conducted for that campaign indicated that our graduates were very charitable but that, on average, we received just 1 percent of their philanthropic dollars. Prior to 2001, there had been only three gifts of over $5 million and 78 of over $1 million, on a cumulative lifetime basis. Most alumni believed that HBS *deserved* their support, but didn't *need* it. Changing that perception, and convincing alumni that their contributions would indeed make a difference, required us to build a compelling case combined with powerful communications. **(See the campaign story below.)** During the campaign, we received 35 gifts of over $5 million and 80 of over $1 million. Quite a change—brought about by explicitly communicating HBS's impact in the world.

THE HBS CAPITAL CAMPAIGN

In 1995, HBS embarked on an effort to reinforce its global relevance by focusing on entrepreneurship, technology, and globalization. Five years later, HBS's Dean Kim Clark set about translating a set of somewhat vague goals into concrete plans, in the context of the challenges and opportunities brought by the dawn of the 21st century. As he explained:

> We stand at an inflection point in history when the demands placed on business and business leaders have never been greater or more complex. This changing world calls for new skills in our graduates and a new standard of leadership in education from Harvard Business School.

It was clear that a significant investment would be required to meet the challenge; HBS would have to launch the first capital campaign in its 94-year history. Five broad initiatives were identified: attract the best students, deepen the learning experience, attract and develop faculty, increase impact and global reach, and renew the residential community. Major projects were identified within each area, with room left for other initiatives that might arise. The price tag: $500 million.

Historically, fundraising at HBS was a relatively low-key activity, dominated by alumni reunion activity. The fundraising approach was what some might call "testosterone-driven"—that is, challenging classes or sections within a class to outdo each other, or offering individuals a menu of gift options to which to attach their names for peer recognition. Giving had increased over the years, but only modestly. And yet its importance was magnified by the fact HBS doesn't receive any U.S. government funding, which is quite unusual for a major institution.

First, there were some myths to dispel about the School's presumed vast resources. A common red herring—the campus's well landscaped grounds—could be defused with humor ("No, it's not true. We do not

THE HBS CAPITAL CAMPAIGN (CONT.)

shampoo the squirrels.") and then following up with facts about the sheer scale and scope of the physical plant, which is far more extensive than many corporate headquarters. To provide full transparency for its numbers-oriented alumni, HBS also published its first annual financial report. Many alums were surprised to learn that the school's income from endowment and gifts represented a relatively small portion of revenues (21 percent). In fact, by design, the HBS economic model was quite market-sensitive, with 21 percent of revenues coming from the MBA program, 23 percent from executive education, 31 percent from publishing, and 5 percent from housing and other sources.

The campaign was targeted to run from 2002 through 2006. As it geared up, a major challenge emerged: the economy. The 9/11 terrorist attacks in 2001 were followed by a global recession. HBS remained financially stable thanks to stringent cost management, but all of its revenue sources were hit. Campaign organizers were concerned: would the larger economic picture hurt the giving environment? As it turned out, the campaign's pre-launch phase exceeded expectations, raising almost $250 million by the end of fiscal 2002 on the strength of some early significant gifts.

Another known challenge, as we headed into the campaign, was improving alumni relations and sharpening up the school's message. A communications firm was engaged before the launch to generate a communications strategy. Based on extensive alumni interviews, the consultants concluded that the school's alumni wanted clear, definite reasons to give, and that communications needed to be on a visceral—not cerebral—level. After testing 15 concept statements, a winner emerged: "The mission of HBS is to educate leaders who make a difference in the world." Previously, the school's central purpose had not been clearly articulated.

THE HBS CAPITAL CAMPAIGN (CONT.)

The campaign's launch event (the "kickoff") included a series of faculty panels on pressing business issues, and was highlighted by an inspirational multimedia presentation featuring a series of personal stories told by people whose lives had been changed through initiatives supported by members of the HBS community:

- A welfare mother trained at the Center for Women in Enterprise—a nonprofit founded by an alumna—who went on to establish a golfing range business and become self-sufficient

- A successful and ambitious Latino Pizza Hut regional manager whose boss—and his boss, and his boss's boss—were all alumni

- A violinist who had trained at the New England Conservatory, which some alumni had helped through a downturn with both financial support and strategic guidance

- A young woman suffering from dystonia whose condition had been relieved by brain implants, in part due to the efforts of an alum who previously had trained in neurosurgery

- A Brazilian paper company, owned by an alumnus, that embraced ecologically sensitive methods to the benefit of both the economy and the environment

From there, we rolled out the campaign to alumni groups in 12 cities. The dean of the school, I and/or development staff followed up with interested individuals; there were thousands of such meetings. Care was taken to address not just individual donors, but their spouses and families as well. The school's leadership, alumni network, faculty, and staff all were called on to support the effort, and were kept engaged throughout. In developing a "case statement," we clarified the rationale for the campaign overall and for each set of initiatives under its umbrella. The campaign afforded a rare opportunity to rally the

THE HBS CAPITAL CAMPAIGN (CONT.)

entire community behind the school and its mission.

The campaign reached its financial goal early, and ultimately generated $600 million—20 percent over goal—compared to the $750 million previously raised through HBS's 92-year history. It also strengthened relations with alumni, and put in place a structure for engaging them on an ongoing basis. One very welcome result, not uncommon in the wake of a highly successful campaign: annual giving at HBS increased by a factor of two.

A call I received from a friend and former HBS section-mate midway through the campaign further reinforced the importance to donors of making a difference.[16] HansJoerg Wyss was a generous donor who had already funded a faculty chair at HBS—as well as 12 others across the country! When he called me, he said that he had been avoiding me; I said, "I noticed." He then added that he didn't want to fund "five chairs," which struck me as an interesting comment. We both knew that chairs were not a priority for HBS at that time, so I took it as an indication of the size of gift he had in mind. I quickly did the math; five chairs were probably worth about $25 million. This was his indirect way of saying, *Be innovative.* If I could prove that he could make a real difference, he might be willing to make a significant gift. I also knew that he understood leverage, the power of multiplying the impact of a gift beyond its direct recipient.

HansJoerg's company had invested heavily in training people how to use its engineered orthopedic products. I thought something to support the school's doctoral program—a priority area of investment for the school—might appeal to him because of its direct impact on teaching and learning, and "ripple effect." I prepared and sent a proposal for an endowment that would fund

---

[16] The large incoming classes at HBS are divided into sections to give students a more intimate—and intense—educational experience.

fellowships and stipends for doctoral students, increased support for field research, new doctoral course development, training in teaching skills, and the renovation of doctoral facilities on campus.

There was silence, then requests for more information, and then more silence. Just over a year after my initial proposal, I received a phone message to meet him in New York at an event being held in his honor by another philanthropic organization. I personally bought a table, and took some doctoral students with me. He met and liked them.

Radio silence again. Several months later, he came to HBS, for more discussion of our doctoral students' work and the program in general. The following week, negotiation of gift agreement terms began. The money soon followed. At the announcement of the gift, HansJoerg commented:

> *The doctoral programs at Harvard Business School have a tremendous influence, not only through the candidates educated here, but through the thousands of students they eventually teach and the millions more who benefit from the*

research and new ideas they generate...I am proud to support this effort.[17]

Ultimately, his willingness to make a significant gift rested on his feeling at an intuitive, gut level that he was helping people who ultimately could make a difference in the world. The lesson for me: patience and persistence!

For some donors, "making a difference" means helping an institution do something it wouldn't otherwise be able to do, or solving a problem that is not currently being addressed. As it turns out, there are many ways to hit that high standard. It may be a matter of scale—for example, marshaling the financial resources needed to fund a new science center at your alma mater. (Laboratories and museums are particularly expensive spaces!) Or it may involve a cause that—for whatever reason—has difficulty attracting funding. So-called "orphan" diseases and stem cell research would qualify: the former don't represent markets large enough to interest pharmaceutical companies; the latter have been cut off from federal funding in recent years. In these and many similar cases, private donors have stepped forward to fill the financial gaps.

---

[17] HBS Alumni Bulletin, December 2004, (http://www.alumni.hbs.edu/bulletin/2004/december/ib_wyss.htm) last accessed 4/15/2011.

Here's a challenge you may well run into: *If you think this is so important, and you have a contribution to make in this field, why aren't you working on it already?*

I've heard that a lot. In one case, I had reached the point where a prospect for a major new Harvard research institute was excited, but wasn't quite ready to ante up. First, he said, he wanted to see some "sweat equity" on the part of Harvard, and a certain amount of progress in the specified direction. This was no small task, and would not be accomplished quickly. In fact, it required lots of nights and weekend work on the part of researchers and some strong institutional championing. Years passed (literally!). I kept the prospect involved, and our discussions continued. The original proposal was refined, and then refined some more. Ultimately, our patience and perseverance was rewarded. The donor funded the entire multi-million dollar initiative—and did so with great enthusiasm.

As I've mentioned before, some individuals may want to get personally involved in your organization and its cause by contributing their time, talent, and networks. For some, it is a way to get to know an organization before deciding whether to make a significant gift. Many expect to remain very active in the life of the organization in the wake of a significant gift. Remember, too, that "personal involvement" can take a variety of forms. John and Pam Humphrey, friends of mine, estimate that they invite between 1,400 and 1,700 people to their home each year for events in support of one cause or another. Their personal and professional networks, and their name recognition and credibility as significant donors, are invaluable to the organizations they support.

Management and fundraising expertise can be especially valuable to smaller nonprofit organizations. John and Pam, for example, were committed to improving the quality of life in their community. They realized that much more of the local population visited the local zoo than attended the ballet and other institutions they had traditionally supported. When John looked into the zoo, he found an organization with all kinds of appeal but which was in terrible shape financially, and had no fundraising activity to speak of. He then asked the obvious question: *Why not raise $2.5 million to support our zoo?* And when no one else stepped forward, John led the (highly successful) effort himself.

In another case, the close friend of a victim of a rare disease was more than happy to donate to an organization established to accelerate the search for a cure. When he also accepted an invitation to join its board, he found it somewhat . . . well . . . *loose* in its management style. Quickly and forcefully, he applied his considerable strategic and financial skills to tighten up the organization's practices. Yes, he supported the effort to conquer the disease. In addition, he knew that as a board member, he was personally accountable for any major wrongdoing on the part of the organization. As a friend (and chronic board member) puts it: *The buck stops here.* Having individuals like that on your board can be both painful and a godsend.

To sum up the main point of this chapter: be prepared to explain, in simple and compelling terms, how a gift from a prospective donor will help change the world. Start with the assumption that this donor is a very savvy individual. What's the story line, and what are the specific giving opportunities within that story line, that might appeal to this person? If it concludes with "no sale," at least you've educated him or her about your organization and cause.

I'll close by citing the example of Strategic Grant Partners, which is a giving consortium of fifteen wealthy families. I find it an especially interesting and innovative example of how donors can assemble and deploy an impressive array of resources—time, talent, treasure, and networks—to make a difference, while concurrently developing mutually satisfying relationships with their grantees. It also illustrates what for your organization is likely to be both a challenge and an opportunity: the growing sophistication of significant donors.

STRATEGIC GRANT PARTNERS

Boston-based Strategic Grant Partners (SGP) was founded in September 2002 by fourteen families with the shared mission of funding great leaders with game changing ideas who could help struggling individuals and families in Massachusetts improve their lives. Joanna Jacobson, a co-founder and Managing Partner, explained its origins as follows:

I wanted to devote my time and my private-sector experience to influence positive change. All of the partners are committed donors who share a common problem. Lacking the time for research and due diligence, we often give to well-known organizations, or in response to requests from friends. Donors soon become overwhelmed by the volume of requests, and underwhelmed by the impact of their donations.

Not unlike work in the private sector, we all started with the conviction that great leaders with game changing ideas are at the crux of success. Yet the nonprofit sector did not typically attract the talent or provide the seed capital necessary to support catalytic leadership.

Our work focuses on education, child welfare, high risk youth and family self-sufficiency, and starts with the conviction that people, when offered incentives and opportunities, can succeed and assume responsibility for their futures. As a country we've lost our way, treating impoverished adults and struggling youth like charity cases, and trying to treat their problems rather than giving them the tools and opportunities to achieve their own success.

SGP describes itself as both a foundation and a pro bono consulting firm. Its model, which has evolved over the years, involves creating close working partnerships with grantees to provide the capital they need to realize their potential as well as strategic support, and implementation assistance. SGP does not accept unsolicited

STRATEGIC GRANT PARTNERS (CONT.)

proposals, instead identifying opportunities through its network and research. It makes a small number of relatively large grants in areas with the potential to bring a promising opportunity to scale, or test something that might have far-reaching implications. Other criteria include outstanding leadership, a viable strategy for long-term sustainability, specific measurable outcomes, and data transparency. Before awarding a grant, SGP goes through an intensive strategic planning process with key players, and does due diligence in the field to get a feel for the organization. It then stays close to grantees, offering ongoing support and useful connections.

Joanna described one educational initiative:

Boston Public Schools (BPS) was a revolving door for new teachers. We asked "What can't you effect, to solve this problem?" The problem was that new teachers were unprepared for an urban teaching environment. BPS leadership was interested in an idea modeled on medical residencies, which had been tested in a small charter school by a school leader named Jesse Solomon. The concept was intriguing so we hired him, helped him develop a strategic plan, and paid for the start-up year and the first two years of program operation with the understanding that BPS would gradually take over the costs.

The Boston Teacher Residency Program (BTR) recruits talented individuals of all ages. In exchange for a three-year commitment, residents participate in a full year master's program and practicum. After an intensive summer institute, they spend the academic year in the classroom with a mentor teacher four days a week, and in the evenings and on Fridays they complete their master's coursework. Upon graduation from the program they earn teacher licensure, a master's degree in teaching, and a job in the Boston Public

STRATEGIC GRANT PARTNERS (CONT.)

Schools.

Since BTR's launch in 2002, BPS's three–year teacher retention rate has climbed from 50 percent to 84 percent. SGP and BTR together helped co-found a national organization, Urban Teacher Residency United, to help other cities replicate the model. Our grant to BTR was $4.3 million since 2002, given in three different phases.

People familiar with SGP credit a large portion of its effectiveness to Joanna's commitment, talent, and hard work. Joanna earned an MBA at HBS, and built a career in consumer marketing and turnarounds. She was President at a multi-hundred- million dollar company. (Other SGP staff includes a co-founder who works part time, two portfolio managers who are consultants by training, and an office manager). Joanna commented:

What gives us the greatest satisfaction is partnering with exceptional social entrepreneurs who have passion, vision and a commitment to outcomes. We value ideas that are truly impactful, capable of altering the trajectory of people's lives. We encourage grantees to focus on the doable, learn and adapt from mistakes, and hold people accountable to their goals. We focus on early stage enterprises, believing that this is where philanthropy can have its greatest impact. Philanthropy should take the risk of testing and proving (or not proving) new approaches. Once the evidence of effectiveness is demonstrated at scale, government should take over, swapping unproven programs with those that work. Unfortunately, government is rarely willing to end commitments to programs that have no demonstrated outcomes. Politics is still too big of an influence in public funding decisions.

STRATEGIC GRANT PARTNERS (CONT.)

Our job is to assist capable leaders with strategy and resources and then to remain a committed partner providing problem solving, block and tackle support and to provide the lens of a friendly devil's advocate as needed. We try not to waste grantees' time with written reports preferring to stay close to the work on an ongoing basis. We demand accountability for outcomes, but we help grantees shape their organizational metrics and the metrics they choose to run their businesses by, are the same ones they report to us.

Collectively, we have committed $50 million to these endeavors. There's no solicitation involved; the people that make up SGP are partners in this work. Our partners participate in more than just donating dollars and decision making. They have provided grantees with connections, ideas and advice. We meet four times a year to propose a grant opportunity. Beforehand, we provide upfront research for our partners, and allow them to vet the grant opportunity directly with the potential grantees. We all vote, and decisions are most often unanimous. It's an opportunity to talk and learn from one another. It has been a generative experience for the group.

CHAPTER 5

WILL THE EXPERIENCE BE SATISFYING TO ME?

Philanthropy is a voluntary transaction. It involves a "give" and a "get." When it comes to donors, the question is: What is the currency? A good feeling? Publicity? Permanent enshrinement? The best seats at a college football game? Being on a committee, with "insider" status? For donors of significant gifts, impact is almost certainly of importance. But beyond that, figuring out what may make the giving experience satisfying for a donor can be a challenge for a fundraiser. Many people don't want to ask for what they want, so it can be a process of divination. You don't want to put them in the position of having to ask; "it"—whatever it is—should be offered in a spirit of thanks.

This process can be complicated, though. You have to be able leave your ego and values aside, even if you may be thinking, "What a jerk for wanting that!" (It's rare, but it happens.) At the same time, you have to preserve the integrity of the institution. Not every donor wish can or should be fulfilled.

I once was approached by someone interested in making a $5 million donation to HBS. The quid pro quo? He wanted his son guaranteed admission. I found that more than a little offensive. But I paused, and asked him how old his son was. He replied "Nine years old." I explained to him that HBS doesn't sell admissions. We didn't get the money.

I want to stress that I'm not talking here just about the formal "thank you's" that mark the closing of the gift transaction—although of course those formalities are important. I'm talking about the entire giving experience. What will make that experience personally satisfying, for this particular donor?

R-E-S-P-E-C-T

One of my favorite fundraising stories concerns Dick Spangler, who at the time that this episode took place was in his sixties and president of the University of North Carolina (UNC) system. A highly accomplished individual who distinguished himself both in business and academia, Spangler previously had served as chairman of the Bank of North Carolina and chairman of the State Board of Education.

Dick's daughter was volunteering at a nursing home, and one day came home with news for him. "Your fourth-grade teacher is a resident there," she said. "She's so proud of you." Dick didn't recognize the woman's name, and they went back and forth several times over her possible identity. Dick continued to draw a blank.

Eventually, Dick went to see this woman who claimed to have been his teacher, and he instantly recognized her. (He had been misled by the name his daughter had told him; the former teacher had married in the interim and taken the name of her husband, now deceased.) They had a nice chat, and Dick thought no more of it. Some weeks later, his daughter came home with more news: "She wants to make a donation to the university." Contemplating his already crowded schedule, Dick sighed inwardly, but resolved to return to the nursing home to accept what he assumed would be a check for a small amount of money.

He found his former teacher all dressed up with her financial adviser at her side. The latter handed Dick a check for $1 million. Seeing his dumbfounded expression, the woman explained that she and her husband had accumulated some money over time, but had no children. She wanted to establish a scholarship fund at the UNC School she had attended. Some years later, when Dick decided to make a legacy gift to UNC, he established a chair at each school in the system—and named the one at her alma mater in her honor.

The main lesson in this story, for me, is about *respect*. By any measure, Dick Spangler was an important and busy guy, but he took the time to meet with his former teacher a second time. And he later honored her memory with one of his own gifts, to the school they both loved. Being respectful to donors is fundamental for success. Hopefully, it comes naturally, and is reciprocal. I should point out that in his role as chair of the HBS campaign— and I'm sure in his other fundraising ventures—Dick also was quick to act if he felt any member of the fundraising team was not being treated with dignity. Respect is a two-way street.

IT'S A JOURNEY

When it comes to raising significant gifts, you're usually not talking about a day trip; you're talking about a lengthy journey. As with any such journey, preparation is needed. You choose your travel companions, and plan your itinerary. It seems straightforward enough: engage a prospect, make a proposal, formalize the gift, and nurture the relationship. In reality, of course, things are more complicated. It can be a long and winding road, with ups and downs. Things can happen unexpectedly, either for better or worse. And at each step of the way, you need to be trying to make the experience satisfying to the donor... whatever that may mean to him or her.

Copyright Grantland Enterprises; www. grantland.net

One of the first things I try to determine, as I'm entering into a donor relationship, is *whom I need to keep happy*. Especially in a family or family-foundation context, it is increasingly rare to find a sole decision-maker when a significant amount of money is on the table. A spouse is likely to be involved, and perhaps other family members, as well—and in many cases, they can make real contributions to the cause. With that in mind, I make it a habit to invite spouses to fundraising events. In many cases, frankly, it's less about getting that spouse excited about the philanthropic opportunity, and more about making sure he or she doesn't veto the endeavor.

Not all families are icebergs—with only a small fraction of their mass visible above the water line—but many are. Keep in mind that the family's influence may be significant when it comes to the size of the gift, the terms of agreement, or the subsequent oversight of its use. In the case of endowed gifts, the role of future generations of the family may also need to be considered. Princeton University learned this the hard way in 2007 when it faced a lengthy and expensive "donor intent" lawsuit by the family of William Robertson. Robertson claimed that the $35 million stock gift made by his parents in 1961 was not being used for the agreed-upon purpose of training students for U.S. government service. Princeton claimed that the fund was established to support the mission of the Woodrow Wilson School of Public and International Affairs, which included other policy-related careers; and that the original agreement gave Princeton control over the use of the money.

When it comes time to make a proposal, you don't want the donor to feel pressured; you want to leave room for dialogue. One common mistake is making the ask too soon. I have seen academic leaders—presidents and deans—act on the assumption that because they have gotten in front of someone, that person "gets it." Not necessarily so! Until you have agreement on the problem, the donor's confidence in your organization, and a concrete proposal, an ask is premature.

The gift idea may be something specific, or it may be a preliminary response to a general "problem." In the latter case, you may want to start by developing a few options for discussion at the conceptual level. In either case, you want to establish a partnership based on a shared vision. For example, when a South American businessman expressed an interest in collaborating with Harvard on something important, my response was, "I don't know how big a dream you're willing to embrace, or your timing. But as an institution, we have the ability to pull together resources and teams to make dreams come true."

Then I set about trying to figure out what that dream might be, and how to operationalize it.

When I reviewed his career, I thought I saw three underlying principles at work: 1) *excellence matters*, 2) *success* (for individuals, institutions, and nations) *must be earned*; and 3) *organizations and societies suffer from a failure to collaborate across borders*. Based on this analysis and our opening conversations, I identified education, science, and health as areas of special interest to him. In an initial proposal letter from Harvard's president, we outlined conceptual ideas for addressing global challenges in each of those areas:

- An institute for developing and disseminating new approaches to promoting effective human development, social integration, and economic productivity, globally

- A fellowship program for developing innovative and skilled public service professionals whose work would result in global economic growth

- An endeavor aimed at addressing the global health challenges that serve as barriers to opportunity and the pursuit of success

Discussions over the next several months culminated in a multi-dimensional program in support of globalization that included student and faculty research on globalization issues, scholarships for advanced degree candidates from South America to study at Harvard, summer experiences abroad for Harvard students, and faculty exchanges. Harvard set up an office in Brazil to facilitate work with local faculty. The price tag: $25 million.

Getting a sense of what dollar range of gift is possible for your donor is important, and—for obvious reasons—somewhat delicate. You want to put a number in front of your donor, but not put him in an awkward position. "This building will cost $50 million" is quite different from, "Will you give $50 million for this building?" If he says, "Are you asking me for $50 million?" you can say, "If you'd like to, we'd be really grateful." Another approach is to say: "To do what we're hoping to do will cost $1 million." You might tack on, "We hope you'll consider a gift that you consider significant." With an overture like this, you'll likely get the information you need to realistically frame a more detailed proposal.

Only now are you prepared for the moment of truth: *the ask*. Think of it as a marriage proposal; you want to be reasonably sure of a positive reception. I used to have a hard-and-fast rule that asks had to be made in person, as much to make the donor feel valued as for communication effectiveness. I still believe that's the best approach for new prospects, as well as for many repeat donors. But after a lot of back and forth, a colleague has convinced me that in certain cases, a "long-distance ask"—even via e-mail—is fine. He finds that some donors with whom he and the institution have longstanding relationships actually prefer the convenience of e-mail. The prerequisite: significant trust on both sides. On balance, though, I believe a live ask is the best approach.

In such cases, how you do it will depend on the individual, as well as the nature of what you're proposing. You'll want him to feel comfortable, and fully satisfied that he is doing the right thing. When and where to meet? What information will he want, in what form? You'll likely have to work around the donor's schedule. Should it be a formal meeting, with slides? Or more casual, perhaps over dinner? Who should participate?

Watch for clues about what the donor wants, and *be flexible* in response. At least two mega-million dollar donors whom I cultivated had no great interest in meeting Harvard's president during the solicitation process. This was a source of great consternation to many of my fundraising colleagues: *Aren't these donors serious?* In fact, they were very serious; they just weren't interested in hierarchy and ceremony. They much preferred to spend time with the academic leaders whom they were being asked to sponsor. My own role became less central during the solicitation process, with me mainly serving in the role of facilitator as the project and proposal took shape. I certainly didn't object to that—so long as the check arrived with the right number of zeros. And it was consistent with our strategy of having multiple connections with donors so that they would always have a link with the institution; fundraisers do come and go.

This will come as no shock, but you won't always get a resounding "yes!" right off the bat. Don't take it personally. Be gracious . . . and *smart*. If you realize that you're getting a "get out of my face!" gift, be grateful and respectful—and get out of the donor's face! Meanwhile, don't slam any doors. Sometimes it just doesn't work out.

Sometimes it doesn't work out in the short term, but does work out longer-term.

Let me be clear here: if you get a definitive "NO!! And don't call me again," take a hint. If you pester someone, you'll risk not only aggravating them, but having them complain about you to their friends. *But* keep them in your file, and hold no grudges if they warm up some day when circumstances change. One HBS donor told me in no uncertain terms that he didn't want to hear from me again; I crossed him off my list. Some time later, he told the HBS dean that he couldn't figure out why I was mad at him: *Why hasn't Howard been in touch?* The dean followed up and seven years later—yes, seven years later— he made a million-dollar gift. You never know... but pay attention to the signals along the way.

Copyright Grantland Enterprises; www. grantland.net

What about a less definitive "no"? What if you hear "maybe," or "I don't think so," or "Sorry, I can't"? In my experience, that may just mean "not now," as opposed to "never." If you feel that the door is still open at least a crack, it's entirely appropriate to ask if you can stay in touch. If they are amenable, you can then go into relationship-nurturing mode. Consider asking them to get involved in a volunteer capacity; this may be well received, especially if they just weren't in a position to make a financial gift at that juncture but do want to support your cause.

Sometimes a donor simply needs more information. Sometimes there are clear—but resolvable—issues to be addressed. Keep in mind, though, that there's a huge difference between a *reason* for not giving and an *excuse*. Do your best to address them. But be alert to the signs of an excuse, and don't waste your time (or his, or hers).

On a fundraising trip to an HBS alum's Florida home, I found him determined to talk about one thing, and one thing only: the parking ticket he had received in the HBS parking lot back in his student days some 30 years earlier. He hadn't, and wouldn't, let go of that. Finally—figuring this was a lost cause—I pointed out that Harvard University, not HBS, controls Harvard's parking lots and issues tickets; offered to write him a check for the cost of the ticket, if that would make him feel better; and suggested that if this one memory was all he had taken away from HBS, then we probably shouldn't be having this discussion. That jolted him into a more positive conversation. And yes, he did eventually make a gift.

An even more extreme—and less successful—example: one of my friends, a very successful volunteer fundraiser, likes to tell what he calls the Peanut Butter Story. Again, it begins with a call on a donor. After some discussion, the donor asked if my friend liked peanut butter.

"Yes," my friend replied.

"Well, then, no money from *me*," the donor shot back.

"Why not?" asked the puzzled fundraiser.

"Well, I wasn't going to give you any anyway, but now I have a *reason*."

In my terminology, that's not a reason, but an excuse. I hope that you (and I!) don't run into too many characters like that.

Sometimes the donor may just need extra time to reflect. Some Harvard development staffers and I met with a donor who had gifted $1 million for each of four years. He was thrilled with the project he was funding. At the meeting, we asked if he would consider doing more. He said "Yes, but..." I quickly interjected "Well, that's better than 'hell, no!'" It turned out that he had a number of philanthropic commitments, and needed to figure out whether he could fit the request into his cash flow.

After the meeting, a development person drafted a letter for me, requesting that the donor add $500,000 a year to his current $1 million gift. I tweaked the letter a bit so that it conveyed three messages in an understated way: first, that we were truly glad he was happy with the work already underway; second, that this was a critical juncture in the history of the project; and third, that if there was any way he could increase or extend his gift, it would be greatly appreciated. Why that approach? I wanted to give him not only a graceful way to say "no," but also a relatively painless way to say "yes." I knew he had the means. Ultimately, he said no—but added five more years to his million-dollar-a-year commitment. Entirely fine by me!

Once the proposal is successfully sold, the next challenge is to translate it into a formal gift agreement. Getting the details right is important for several reasons: to show that you take the gift seriously, to achieve a true meeting of the minds between the donor and the institution, and to preclude the possibility of any future problems. With permanent endowments, a common (and understandable) error is the assumption on the part of the donor of "permanence" under all circumstances, forever. Things *do* change. Buildings live their useful life and get taken down. (That was the problem faced by Brandeis University as it prepared to demolish an old science center to make way for a new one, prompting a lawsuit by the old center's donor family.) Things that are important in one era—say, a professorship in railroading, which was a real-life example from HBS—become less important in subsequent eras.

And what if a prominent donor is convicted of a felony? Do you really want his name emblazoned indefinitely on the lintel of one of your buildings?

"Out clauses" are one solution. Think of them as a sort of prenuptial agreement (a concept which many donors are already aware of and comfortable with). They basically specify how both parties will behave if and when the assumptions behind the gift no longer pertain.

Processing the gift can be simple or complicated, depending on the specific circumstances. But the twin watchwords should be: *do it right*, and *do it fast*. I was less than pleased when a gift from my family foundation was incorrectly attributed to me personally; the error could have caused me tax issues. Another time, my wife Fredi and I attended a wedding where the couple had requested donations to a summer camp in lieu of gifts. We sent off a nice check in the couple's name. Some weeks later, we received a letter from the camp saying they didn't know who those people—the newlyweds—were, or how to contact them. Oops!

To continue the marriage metaphor: Wedded bliss generally requires as much effort as courtship and marriage, and sometimes even more. A donor expects, and *deserves,* excellent financial stewardship. At a minimum, annual accounting of funds is essential, in an accurate, easy-to-understand, and completely transparent manner. The donor should be able to see where his money is going—for example, in terms of total dollars spent by specific programs. As a fundraiser, you need to be watchful on behalf of your donor, as well as your institution. I once noticed that a donor's gift had been mishandled. I had it taken care of, and then I went to the donor and "turned us in." I told him that we had screwed it up, found the error and fixed it, and that we were very sorry. The donor expressed his gratitude for our forthrightness, and ultimately went on to make more gifts.

The donor needs to be kept up to date on the organization's work, accomplishments, plans, and challenges. One way to do that is to get her directly involved as a volunteer, ideally in a leadership position. On the flip side, the institution needs to keep up to date on the donor and her life, with an eye to determining when the timing might be right to approach her for another gift. Obvious, but important to remember: you're much more likely to get a positive reception if she continues to feel good about the work she and her money are doing, and how she's being treated.

Also obvious: *say "thank you."* Closing the deal may or may not be part of leadership's job, but thanking always is. Express your gratitude for the donor's commitment to your cause and confidence in your organization. I find a handwritten note goes a long way, even if most people can't read my handwriting. Offer public acknowledgement in a way that is comfortable and meaningful for him, to the best of your ability. In the case of the South American donor's globalization gift, there were formal announcements. We later got all the people he was supporting together, and showcased some of the initiative's work. That acknowledgement of his contribution—and, of course, signs of progress "on the ground"—reassured him that his money was being well spent.

Don't wait for the occasion of the gift to say "thank you." Say it early and often, and with sincerity: "For meeting with me ... for helping me understand more about what you're doing philanthropically... for your interest in what we're doing ..." And here's the one that fundraisers are least likely to extend, and which most donors are genuinely surprised and pleased to hear: "Thank you for all the other good work you're doing in the world." (A few specifics can go a long way, here.) Remember that philanthropy is not a competition. A contribution to the New York-based Posse Foundation— which offers four-year, full-tuition scholarships to public high school students who might otherwise be overlooked by traditional college selection processes—may well benefit SummerSearch kids. Why wouldn't SummerSearch celebrate the good works of the Posse Foundation?

IT SHOULD BE *MUTUALLY* SATISFYING

Your relationship with a donor should be just as satisfying for you and the institution as for him. It can (and often should) be an ongoing partnership—a joint pursuit of opportunities to make a difference. If as you consider a potential donation, you have some doubts—for example, if the proposed gift isn't truly aligned with your mission, as discussed earlier—maybe you and your institution should reconsider. Painful as it may be, sometimes it's best for your institution to say "no." Some people are surprised to hear me say it, but the fact is, a big part of the fundraising job is learning when (and how!) to say "no."

That said, you can still try to preserve the relationship in the short run (maybe suggest a smaller gift more suited to your needs) or the long run (earn credibility and trust by offering assistance with finding another worthy cause). Most prospective donors appreciate candor, firmness, and—as noted in earlier chapters—*respect*.

Copyright Grantland Enterprises; www. grantland.net

"The gift that keeps on taking" is another example. Let's say a donor funds the establishment of a center at an educational institution, with a plaque bearing his name. Then what? What new donor is likely to contribute the money necessary to sustain it in the future? What if someone (generously) pays for the construction of a new recreation center, but doesn't make provisions for its operating costs? If the local community gets stuck with that open-ended commitment—without ever being asked about it—is that fair, or sustainable?

A third example is the "hidden-agenda" donation. Sometimes donors are not so much interested in your cause as they are in being affiliated with your institution for their own benefit. That's particularly true for brand-name institutions. That may be benign, or it may not be. An example of the latter situation involved a family who tried for years to make a large donation to HBS. The problem was that the proposed gift was basically a marketing ploy: they wanted to be able claim an affiliation with the School to promote their for-profit business. The issue is becoming a legal as well as moral one, as the rules change (e.g., the IRS is focusing increased attention on the benefits donors get from the organizations they support).

The individuals involved in fundraising—yes, including you—should also feel satisfaction from their donor interactions, and the overall fundraising effort. In all of my fundraising experience, I have run into only a few total jerks. In each of those cases, I decided it was in neither my or the organization's interests to pursue those relationships.

At one of my fundraising talks, a nonprofit executive shared the story of a donor who was insisting that she (the executive) first disclose exactly how much she, personally, was contributing to her organization. She didn't want to, feeling it was an invasion of her privacy. *What should I do,* she asked? I suggested that she inform the donor that she didn't feel comfortable providing that information, and let the chips fall where they might. I never heard how that story turned out, but if no gift came out of the interaction, it was probably no great loss. Jerks make bad partners.

Ideally, each individual will feel like a respected and valued member of the fundraising team. As an aside, I maintain that *everyone* in the organization is, or should be, a "fundraiser" broadly defined. There's simply no better advertisement for your cause than an enthusiastic, articulate staff member who's eager to tell your story to anyone who's willing to listen. And there's nothing better than when everyone in the organization—not just the formal fundraisers—feel responsible for its success. One example: 57 percent of Mount Auburn Hospital's active medical staff is part of the Physicians' Leadership Circle, donating at least $1,000 each year. Including physician giving at all levels, that number climbs to 61 percent.

Let me close with a checklist that summarizes the key steps involved in the journey of significant fundraising (see **Table 5-1**), and illustrate those steps with a fun story about a former student of mine.

TABLE 5-1: RAISING MONEY: A RECAP FOR FUNDRAISING LEADERSHIP

ENGAGE THE PROSPECT	MAKE A PROPOSAL	FORMALIZE THE AGREEMENT	NURTURE THE RELATIONSHIP
Get to know everything about your prospect	*Plan for the ask, which you'll make personally*	*Refine proposal (as needed)*	*Provide financial stewardship*
- basic data	- time, place, setting	- watch out for traps	- annual accounting
- what the donor	- right people to	(motives, etc.)	- other reporting
cares about	involve		
- what "language"		*Develop terms of*	*Communicate the*
she speaks	*Satisfy your*	*agreement*	*impact*
- how much	*prospect that*	- financial terms	*of the gift*
personal	- you do important	- recognition	- "show and tell"
involvement is	work	- out clauses	events
desired	- you are well	- governance	- talent and
- role of	managed		beneficiaries
spouse/family	- a gift will make a	*Get them signed*	
- open book or	difference		*Get/keep the*
poker game	- it will be a	*Acknowledge the*	*donor involved in*
	satisfying	*gift*	*the organization*
	experience	- institutional leaders	- multiple "touch
		- press release/other	points"
			- regular
Educate the	*Describe gift*	*Process the gift*	communications
prospect about	*idea(s)*	- accurately	- volunteer
your organization,	- tailor it to your	- in a timely manner	positions
from his	prospect's passions		
perspective	- if a general		*Keep up to date on*

ENGAGE THE PROSPECT	MAKE A PROPOSAL	FORMALIZE THE AGREEMENT	NURTURE THE RELATIONSHIP
- focus on things the donor wants to impact - use the donor's language	concept, have a few options - get a sense of possible gift size		*the donor,* with an eye toward gift openings
Determine what you have that might interest your prospect - match between the donor's vision and your mission - ability to tackle a problem the donor wants to solve	*Determine next steps, keep the ball in your court* - be clear at the end of each meeting - conclude with "I've got some further work to do. I'll be back to you then."		*Stay in touch with the donor* to show you care
Develop a "hip pocket" of gift ideas - know the cost of each - don't pull out your list!	*Say thank you for* - the meeting - interest in your work - the donor's other philanthropic work - anything else you can think of!		

THE PENNY AND ROE STAMPS STORY

E. Roe Stamps IV was an HBS Class of 1974 alumni, and one of my former students. The founding managing partner of Summit Partners, a private equity firm, he had achieved considerable financial success, and had a strong track record of generous giving to education-related causes, including the Roe Stamps Fields for sports at his undergraduate alma mater, Georgia Tech. At HBS, he had served as an alumni adviser, but his donations to date had totaled just $16,000.

Our campaign team had Roe high on its list of early prospects. Our thinking was that he might be interested in something technology-related, given that that was where he had made his money, or in scholarships, because he had been a scholarship recipient at HBS. I approached Roe in 2000, during the "quiet phase" before the campaign's official launch. It was a low-key visit to his home. "I just happen to be in Florida," I told him on the phone, "and I'd love to see you." For reasons explained earlier in this chapter, I took a younger development officer with me.

During the one-hour meeting, Roe indicated that he was interested in doing something that would affect students' lives. He also gave the impression that he wouldn't be averse to having his name on something. As I was about to leave, Roe said: "Send me something." What ensued, over the next two years, were fifteen-minute meetings here and there and a series of very different proposals: a fund for the innovative use of technology, scholarships, a professorship, a multi-media lab, and so on.

Each proposal was met with no response, or "it's not quite right." There were long silences. Roe came to be known as "our elusive friend." Finally, in a last-ditch effort, the team put together a proposal related to the renovation of Baker Library. The library's reading room was the focus. Why? There were only so many naming opportunities left; of which the reading room was one. We knew that Roe's wife Penny was deeply involved in historic preservation, and the reading room was a strong example of the McKim, Mead & White architectural firm's work. It was highly visible; students went there

THE PENNY AND ROE STAMPS STORY (CONT.)

every day. It required a technology investment; the reading room of 1974 didn't meet the needs of the 21st century. And there was a large aesthetic component: the plan was to restore the room to its original 1926 appearance, which would involve restoring skylights painted out and covered up for blackout purposes during World War II, and refinishing the proud-but-worn woodwork. We figured we could ask for $5 million.

Part of the process involved showing Roe and Penny what the project would ultimately yield. There were pictures of the original room, architectural designs and plans. Baker was already torn apart, so they could tour the gutted building and visualize the potential of the project. Roe and Penny became increasingly excited. But, still there was no commitment. I became increasingly frustrated with myself. I couldn't make it work, and I couldn't figure out why. But in hindsight, my contribution was to keep calling him and keep the thing alive.

In 2004, I arranged for Roe to meet with the school's dean and Dick Spangler, the Campaign's Chair. (Sometimes it takes the big guns to close the deal.) The ultimate gift comprised $12 million for the "Penny and Roe Stamps Reading Room," as well as a current-use gift of $1 million for student fellowships, from the couple's charitable foundation. I wasn't involved in the formalization of gift terms, but did assist with thank-you notes from both the school and campaign leadership, as well as press releases.

Roe was not intimately involved in the restoration process, but was very pleased with the results. The reading room's re-opening in 2005 was celebrated with a party for 100 people. As Roe's class notes in the alumni magazine subsequently reported: "During the presentation, Roe quipped that this was his first time in the reading room, ever. Acting Dean [Jay] Light, however, refuted this assertion, having seen Roe sleeping in the reading room on many occasions between 1972 and 1974."

A great outcome, infused with good spirits. In part for those reasons— I like to think—Roe's involvement in school activities subsequently increased significantly.

CHAPTER 6

BEING A FUNDRAISING LEADER

In this final chapter, I'd like to reflect on the role of a fundraising leader. What defines "success?" What can you do, really, to make an impact? What are some of the important things that you should try to keep in mind, as you go about your work?

WHAT IS "SUCCESS"?

As I explained earlier, research indicates that there are four dimensions of enduring success. As it turns out, these four dimensions map quite well onto the challenge of fundraising leadership. (See **Figure 6-1**) Here's an interesting hypothesis, which I've become convinced is true: *Fundraising is one of the few activities in which you get to accomplish all four "success dimensions" at once.* Through fundraising, I can partner with friends and colleagues—and donors—to accomplish things that will have a positive impact on the world around me, now and into the future.

FIGURE 6 - 1 SUCCESS IN FUNDRAISING LEADERSHIP

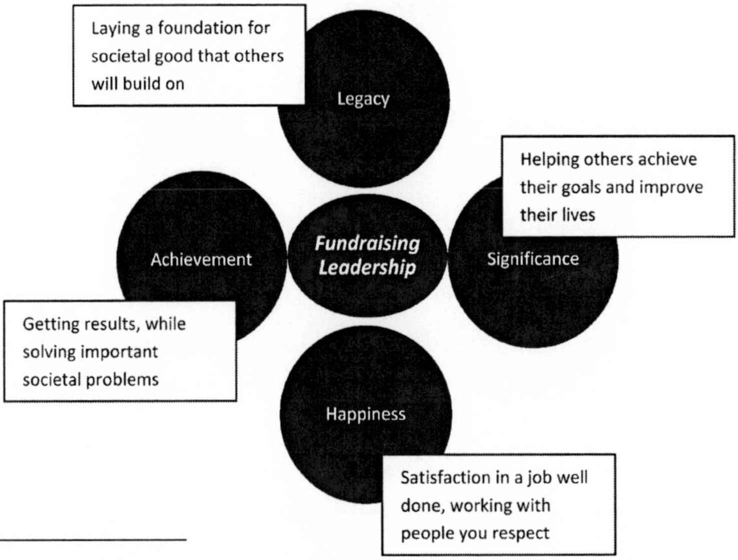

Source: Adapted from *Just Enough: Tools for Creating Success in Your Work and Life*

WHAT CAN YOU DO?

What does being a fundraising leader mean, on a practical level? How can you contribute to the organization you are championing? To some degree, it's Leadership 101, with some special and important applications. More specifically, you can:

- *Create a shared vision for success.* That includes agreement on mission and goals, and also on "how things work around here." It involves communication and consensus-building among multiple stakeholders.

155

- *Accept responsibility for the financial health of the organization.* This may not be your sole responsibility. And yet, as an individual, you can bring a mix of resources to bear—networks, knowledge, and money—to ensure that the organization is smart and transparent about its financials.

- *Ensure that fundraising plans are ambitious but realistic.* Fundraising can play an important role in a nonprofit's economics—but only if it is well thought through, and linked to the organization's mission, goals, and concrete needs.

- *Take the competitive landscape into account.* Other people are likely to see the same social needs as you. Are you doing the same thing differently (and better)? Are they doing things you want to do? Are you competing when you should be cooperating? Maybe you should partner on a project, or create a strategic alliance, or even merge.

- *Build competencies on every dimension.* This includes doing what you say you will, building and maintaining an effective operation, constantly growing the management strength of your organization, and—especially—dealing well with donors.

- *Ensure that fundraising plans are well executed.* Fundraising requires good processes and effective teams.

- *Ensure that resources are available to everyone.* What do people need to do their job well? (Remember: good and timely information, and the freedom to make decisions, are just as important as the right tools.)

- *Remove impediments to performance.* Is there a fundraiser on your team who hoards his prospects? Does your organization suffer from "silo thinking?" Do you have bureaucratic procedures that inhibit customer responsiveness? If these or other roadblocks are getting in your way, take action!

- *Set ethical standards and norms.* There are, of course, the big things, like not violating antitrust policy or stealing. But, there also are the daily things, like not letting people be disrespectful, not wasting precious resources, and saying thank you... and *meaning* it.

Because philanthropy includes so many distinct roles, there are many ways that you as an individual may be able to contribute—and most likely, you can wear more than one hat. As a board member, for example, you may be actively engaged in the organizational leadership activities described above. You may be directly involved in fundraising activities—leading volunteers or making solicitations. Through your own approach to giving, you may serve as a role model for other philanthropists. You may be a facilitator of fundraising—that is, bringing the right combination of people and organizations together for a win/win. Any and all of these roles can leverage your time, talent, treasure, and networks.

SOME THINGS TO REMEMBER

Over the years, through personal experience and observation of good and not so good practices, I've learned a few things about being effective and comfortable in the role of a fundraising leader. Here are my top five:

1. **It's not about you.** Fundraising shouldn't be about you personally, or even about your institution. It should be about *what your organization can do in the world*, in partnership with a donor. Your role is catalyst and facilitator. Because you are representing a mission, *you are not begging.* You can and should be proud of the work you are doing. You are making the world a better place, and giving other people the opportunity to join you in that effort.

2. **Everyone's a fundraiser.** Your organization, top to bottom, is a sales team. Because critical donor interactions can begin with anyone, every staff member and volunteer must believe in your mission, and feel a part of fundraising efforts—even if that's not in their formal job description.

3. **You're the model.** Look at your own attitudes and behaviors, because people are taking their cues from you. Remember: a leader is someone whom people *want* to follow. That's especially important to remember when volunteers are involved.

4. **To be good leader, listen.** That also holds for donor interactions. I like how my grandmother put it: "God gave you two ears and one mouth for a reason. And, if you try to talk out of both sides of your mouth to make up for it, that won't work."

5. **It should be fun!** If it isn't, you're playing the wrong role, or not doing it right. I have a horror of cold calls; I like lots of information. Well, the people around me understand this, and help me with it. An executive director I know is fabulous at generating excitement and winning supporters, but can't make an ask to save his life. Again, he gets the help he needs: a development officer is always close at hand when it comes time to make that ask.

Conclusion

YOUR PHILANTHROPIC JOURNEY

Assuming that you've found some useful ideas, techniques, or tools in the previous chapters, you may also find the brief recap at the beginning of this chapter helpful. And I'd like to leave you with some thoughts on the most important question for fundraising leadership, *why do it?* Is fundraising more than a job? How, and why?

A RECAP

Answering the *four major questions* introduced at the outset of this book has been my central focus. But underlying those four discussions has been an emphasis on the *entrepreneurial* and *donor-centered* perspective that I strongly recommended for most nonprofits engaged in fundraising. And, throughout, I have tried to stress the special challenges and opportunities of *fundraising leadership*.

Let me bring those elements together in one summary chart (see **Table C-1**). It presents some of the key lessons I've tried to convey, and—taking that idea one step further—includes a set of related questions that you may want to ask yourself, on your philanthropic journey.

TABLE C-1: GETTING TO GIVING: A RECAP

Theme	Key Points	Questions for Leaders
Entrepreneurial perspective	• Resources are always in imbalance (demand exceeding supply). • Resources go beyond money (time, talent, networks), and will need to be negotiated.	• What is the opportunity? • What are the resources required? • Why would others collaborate with me (give/get)?
Donor-centered perspective	• It's always about the donor. You may not do what he says, but it's important to understand him. • Donors are busy with other commitments. You're not the only thing they care about.	• Do I really know the person well enough (often underestimated)? • Who is the real decision maker (person, spouse, kids, advisors)?

Theme	Key Points	Questions for Leaders
Question 1: Are you doing important work?	• "Important to me" will vary by age, political leanings, life experience, competing claims, etc. • It must be important to you, too. Fundraising is a job with psychic income.	• Why should the donor see us as important (versus "nice to have")? • How can we communicate our importance? • How will we know we've done what we said we would (measures of success)?
Question 2: Are you well managed?	• Donors don't want to waste time and money. • You can't do it all; focus on the doable and stick to priorities. • Be totally transparent about your finances.	• Does everyone understand the economics? • What skills do we need to manage the organization effectively?
Question 3: Will my gift make a difference?	• No general statements; be very specific about the opportunity. • Be clear on impact and outcomes.	• How can we communicate "bang for the buck?" • How can we demonstrate that something has changed?

Theme	Key Points	Questions for Leaders
Question 4: Will the experience be satisfying to me?	• It's a voluntary transaction, with "gives and gets" • Different people want different things from philanthropy. • Details matter (e.g., timely invoices).	• What will make the experience satisfying to this person? • Does the whole organization understand the importance of that? • Do we say "thank you" enough?
Fundraising leadership	• Leadership must lead • Leadership must manage • Leadership must facilitate hard choices	• Do we have a shared vision? Are people excited about it? • Are we being ambitious but realistic? • How can we be the best at what we do? • Do we know when — and how — to say "no?"

Yes, fundraising is hard work, and it can be challenging in ways that are both predictable and unpredictable. *But the rewards can be huge.* This is the game: finding others like you—who care passionately about your cause—and encouraging them to play with you to make a significant and positive difference in the world. Dealing with those individuals can and should be inspiring. And, if you keep your focus on your organization's mission, you can leverage your own time and talent into something far beyond what you, or they, could do alone.

Are you convinced that fundraising is a path well worth taking? Are you convinced that you can be effective at it, and have fun doing it? I hope so, and I hope that this short book has least helped nudge you in those directions.

Philanthropy is powerful! But don't take my work for it. Individuals from Aristotle to Maya Angelou have spoken of the power of philanthropy, in language far more moving than I can muster. So I'll close with a few borrowed thoughts that I find inspirational, in the hope that they will inspire you, too. (See **Table C – 2**)

TABLE C-2: REFLECTIONS ON PHILANTHROPY

You make a living by what you get. You make a life by what you give.
- **Winston Churchill**

One must know not just how to accept a gift, but with what grace to share it.
- **Maya Angelou**

A man's true wealth is the good he does in this world.
- **Mohammed**

And now abideth faith, hope, charity, these three; but the greatest of these [is] charity.
- **King James Bible, 1 Corinthians 13:13**

I am afraid the only safe rule is to give more than we can spare... If our charities do not pinch or hamper us, they are too small. There ought to be some things we should like to do and cannot do because our charitable expenditures exclude them.
- **C. S. Lewis**

To give away money is an easy matter and in any man's power. But to decide to whom to give it and how large and when, and for what purpose and how, is neither in every man's power nor an easy matter.
- **Aristotle**

It is one of the most beautiful compensations of this life that no man can sincerely try to help another without helping himself...Serve and thou shall be served.
- **Ralph Waldo Emerson**

If you want happiness for an hour, take a nap.
If you want happiness for a day, go fishing.
If you want happiness for a year, inherit a fortune.
If you want happiness for a lifetime, help somebody.
- **Chinese proverb**

I don't know what your destiny will be, but one thing I do know: the only ones among you who will be really happy are those who have sought and found how to serve.
- **Albert Schweitzer**

He who allows his day to pass by without practicing generosity and enjoying life's pleasures is like a blacksmith's bellows – he breathes but does not live.
- **Sanskrit Proverb**

Never doubt that a small group of thoughtful, committed citizens can change the world. Indeed, it is the only thing that ever has.
- **Margaret Mead**

Unless someone like you cares a whole awful lot, nothing is going to get better. It's not.
- **Dr. Seuss, from The Lorax**

I've always respected those who tried to change the world for the better, rather than just complain about it.
- **Michael Bloomberg**

The progress of the world will call for the best that all of us have to give.
- **Mary MacLeod Bethune**.

If you want to change the world, be that change.
- **Mohandas Ghandi**

ACKNOWLEDGEMENTS

So many people have contributed to the quality of my experience in fund raising, the shaping of my thinking about philanthropy, and the writing of this book that any list would be incomplete. The usual author's words apply – those listed are not responsible for errors, omissions, and crazy ideas – but each person listed below and many more have helped me in his or her own way. Here is my attempt to acknowledge their special contributions:

To my family:
First, to my wife Fredi, whose passion behind SummerSearch and other worthy causes has driven me forward, and to the rest to my family who put up with drafts, questions and inattention.

To those who helped create this book:
Shirley Spence, Jeff Cruikshank, Bob Reiss, and Jereann Zann.

To those wise and great philanthropists whose stories are reflected in the book (whether identified or not):
Dick and Merideth Spangler, HansJoerg Wyss, Jorge Paulo and Susanna Lemann, the late Frank Batten, Bill

Bose, Joe and Kathy O'Donnell, Jim Gipson, the late John Hobbs, Pam and John Humphrey, Joanna Jacobsen, Ellen Simmons and the late Matt Simmons, L.E. and Ginny Simmons, and Roe and Penny Stamps.

To my mentors in the art of leadership and philanthropy:

Bill Poorvu, Jordan Baruch, Beth and Seth Klarman, the late Isaac Auerbach, Anne Avis, Kay Bucksbaum, Howard Cox, Ian Cumming, Ray Gilmartin, Amos and Barbara Hostetter, Farla and the late Chet Krentzman, Bob and the late Ruth Halperin, Ed Hajim, Rod and Beverly Hawes, Jim Heskett, the late John Matthews, Warren McFarlan, Rona and Richard Menschel, Arthur Rock, Len Schlesinger, Camilla Smith, and John Whitehead.

To my HBS deans, and the leaders of other charities that I admire and have served:

John McArthur, Kim Clark, Jay Light, Nitin Nohria , my scoutmaster the late Fritz Balmer, the late Ken Bergin, Lisa Blumenthal, Jeanette Clough, the late James Faust, John Herrmann, Kevin Klose, Wayne Klockner, Ron McAdow, Jack Meyer, Linda Mornell,   Antoine van Agtmael, and Vivian Schiller.

To friends and colleagues with whom I have worked in this pasture including:

Michael Chu, Angela Crispi, Dwight and Loretto Crane, Jean Cunningham, Jorge Dominguez, Drew Faust, Allen and Jane Grossman, Myra Hart, Cile Hicks, Steve Hyman, Don Ingber, Rob Kaplan, Herman (Dutch) Leonard, Scott Malkin, Doug Melton, Mike Roberts, Kim Saal, Bill Sahlman, Mal Salter, Eric Sinoway, Larry Summers, and Marshall Wolf.

To the great fundraisers from so many organizations who have taught, prodded, helped, guided, argued with and supported me:

Denise Rossman, Susan Lyons, Josh Merrow, Donella Rapier, Scott Abell, Wendy Baker, Nancy Boccia, Dick and Bill Boardman, Michael Boland, Edward Buckbee , Toni Carbone, Kerry Cietanno, Alice Crawford, Garry Emmons, Christine Fairchild, Stephanie Goff Governali, Ellen Greenfield, Sarah Hall, Susan Hamilton, Ralph James, MaryjaneKubler, Teresa Laffey, Julie Anne McNary, Stephanie Noone, Stephen Player, Jack and Tom Reardon, Katie Rutledge, Lisa Marks Schwarz, Janet Straus, Christine Sullivan, Roger Thompson, Karl Wirka, and Howard Wolf.

I am deathly afraid that by the unintentional omission of a name, I will offend someone. Therefore, finally, I express gratitude to all those who remain anonymous, but have facilitated my learning and sharing of that learning. This includes so many who have contributed generously to causes that I care about, and helped me to learn about significant gifts though their example.

To all, I say THANK YOU!!!

AUTHOR BIOGRAPHIES

Howard Stevenson has been a donor and a fundraiser for most of his life. He believes in "giving back" through financial and nonfinancial (expertise and experience) contributions to nonprofit organizations. He has served as vice provost of Harvard University, senior associate dean of Harvard Business School (HBS), chair of the Harvard Business School Press, chair of National Public Radio, chair of Sudbury Valley Trustees, a trustee of the Massachusetts Nature Conservancy, and a member of the board of both the Boston Ballet and Mount Auburn Hospital. In all of these organizations, fundraising was an important part of the strategy. He has personally touched gifts totaling many hundreds of million dollars, and has led the teams that secured some of the largest gifts in these organizations' histories. These significant gifts ranged from tens of thousands to more than $100 million.

In his other lives, Stevenson has been an entrepreneur, professor and author. He was the founder and first president of the Baupost Group, Inc., which manages partnerships investing in liquid securities for wealthy families. He now serves as co-chair of the Advisory Board of Baupost LLC, a $21 billion registered investment company. His HBS legacy, in addition to having touched the lives of thousands of students, is the establishment of its entrepreneurship program. Upon his recent retirement, a chair was named in his honor. Stevenson also is a prolific author, having published eleven books, and hundreds of articles and case studies.

Shirley Spence's interests and work span the business and nonprofit worlds. After graduating from Dartmouth College, she became a high school teacher. She later earned a master's degree in educational administration, planning and social policy from the Harvard Graduate School of Education. Her first foray into business was as a product manager with Procter & Gamble Canada. She subsequently moved into management consulting, becoming a partner at Mercer Management Consulting (now Oliver Wyman). While there, she assisted the Boston Public Schools as a pro bono consultant. Her private consulting has included an initiative in Senegal, Africa aimed at private enterprise development. As a research associate at the Harvard Business School, she has written over fifty case studies and other materials, most recently focusing on "building a business in the context of a life" in for- and nonprofit settings.

How to Order and Customize *Getting to Giving*

Individual sales.
Getting to Giving is available through amazon.com in print, hard cover or kindle format.

Bulk sales.
Special discounts (10 – 40%) are available on purchases of over fifty copies.

Customized editions. For institutional customers interested in distributing copies to their constituents, you can add your name and logo to the cover, and insert one page of text (letter from leadership, information on donating, etc.) for an additional fee.

For bulk sales and customization, contact the publisher:

Timberline LLC
P.O. Box 639
Belmont, MA 02478

toll-free line: 855-407-4158
international line: 617-945-5724
Email: gettingtogiving@gmail.com

INDEX

175

PRAISE FOR *GETTING TO GIVING*

"As someone who gives money but does not like to raise money, I came away from this book with a very different perspective about how fundraising. As Howard Stevenson points out, it can give both the donor and the fundraiser a sense of achievement, significance, legacy and happiness, as they engage one another in the process of asking for and giving money. Howard's joy in fundraising is infectious, and his book is engaging and actionable."

- Ray Gilmartin, former Chairman, President & CEO, Merck & Company

"Over many years, I have read many books about fundraising. Almost all of them were written by professional fundraisers. None were written by donors. Howard Stevenson has made the money, donated the money, and helped raise more. This is a very unusual convergence, almost unique.

- Dick Spangler, former President, University of North Carolina and former Chair, National Gypsum

"As Howard Stevenson outlines so brilliantly, though fundraising is both art and science, there is a method at the heart of every 'ask.' This book is essential for anyone who has to ask for anything. In a totally accessible and nuanced volume, Stevenson presents in clear detail the steps necessary for success. Your prospects will read this... you should, too."

- Mark Edwards, President, Edwards & Company and Executive Director, Opportunity Nation

"Stevenson's enthusiasm and sense of the honor of the calling of being a fundraiser - one of the great opportunities of a professional life, as he presents it - permeate this book. It is a personal and intimate account that will profoundly affect people who read it – and people who are struggling to be good fundraisers – think about what they do, why they do it, and how to do it."

- Herman ("Dutch") Leonard, Professor of Business Administration (Harvard Business School), Professor of Public Sector Management (John F. Kennedy School of Government), and co-chair of the HBS Social Enterprise Initiative

"This book is wonderful. I could REALLY have benefited from reading it before I started at NPR! I looked for something like it when I started as CEO, to no avail. I predict that it will be a 'must read' for anyone coming into - or even already in - a nonprofit that raises money."

- Vivian Schiller, Chief Digital Officer, NBC and former CEO, National Public Radio

CPSIA information can be obtained at www.ICGtesting.com
Printed in the USA
LVOW082358260112

265755LV00001B/21/P